WOMEN'S RIGHTS

Civil And Moral Laws

Hassan Sadr

Revised Edition

ISBN-10: 1481057944
EAN-13: 978-1481057943

Library of Congress Control Number: 2013908347
CreateSpace Independent Publishing Platform
North Charleston, South Carolina

Preface

The original book was first published as a dissertation for an advanced law degree at Tehran University in 1941. It was reprinted several times in the 60's after its academic appeal made it required reading for law students. This translation is based on latest updated version, 5th edition, 1977.

The topic of women's rights, despite its significant advances in recent decades, remains an important issue of our time. This book offers a fresh perspective on this subject in light of the key social issues of all societies. The idea of allowing a woman to be the natural leader of society by controlling the quality of its membership is refreshing.

From the dawn of civilization, woman has been considered *the* critical component of a family. Woman gives birth to a child, nourishes her child with her milk and blood, and nurtures her children for many years after birth. The prime organizer of a family, the author concludes, is therefore the mother of the children who ensures the stability of the family and validates the idea that well nurtured children greatly contribute to a healthy society. Clearly, the author believes the mother's full participation in such a lengthy process, from childhood to adulthood, is a necessary condition for delivering healthy and fit individuals to society. He further asserts that such society will be healthy, just and peaceful. The significance of safeguarding the rights of women is so critical to the author that the key purpose of family formation, namely, reproduction may otherwise be seriously undermined. The protection of women's rights is a natural pre-requisite for such a society where the law is truly blind in protecting the rights of its members without distinctions or exception.

During a recent episode of *The Colbert Report,* the host interviewed Anne-Marie Slaughter, a Professor of Politics and International Affairs at Princeton University, about her recently published article in the Atlantic Monthly: Why Women Can't Have It All. The debate was about career and family: Women who feel overwhelmed with too much housework and childcare while pursuing a career.

Colbert had a serious point to make: "I'm a parent, you're a parent, you can't have it all, but I can have it all. What is the thing that's different about you?"

Slaughter was more than ready to answer,

"Women are still doing two thirds of the housework and two-thirds of the childcare. Women who have managed to be both mothers and top professionals are superhuman, rich, or self-employed."

Part I of the book discusses the evolution of man's general perception of social status and, in particular, woman's role in a family among various primitive tribes and ancient societies. A major portion of this part of the book is devoted to comparative study of man's psychology and his thought process in different parts of the world. Many stories confirm that the cruelty of men against women, irrespective of the region of the world or the prevailing culture, had its roots in poverty and destitution. Investigation of natural behaviour and habits of different kinds of animals with respect to the natural reproduction process reaffirms that man's cruel behaviour towards woman as compared to animals was inversely proportional to their level of intelligence.

Part II addresses the core social issues of reproduction: Marriage, divorce and distribution of inheritance that are necessary for upbringing of future members of society. There is an extensive and detailed discussion of comparing moral laws with those of mostly European societies. The law of nature and its mechanistic properties as applied to reproduction process are considered the guide for certain moral issues. As an example, the social aspects of natural processes of the reproduction of humans are discussed from the points of view of both civil and moral law. The book explores the grounds for divorce and identifies the circumstances that make it unavoidable. Although divorce is considered harmful to formation of a healthy society, its application is allowed under certain conditions that are now practiced in most countries. The final topic is a comprehensive discussion on how and why inheritance as well as its influence on the entire reproduction process, is so closely linked to societies' cultural background.

September 2013, Boston

Mahmoud Sadre

About the Author

Hassan Sadr (1907-1985) was born in Esfahan, Iran. His early education was influenced by the French school program (*Alliance*) in Esfahan as well as private studies on philosophy under the supervision of his older brother, a well known authority in Islamic philosophy and a political activist, who died in 1936. Hassan Sadr received his law degree with honors from Tehran University in 1933 and later his Doctorate in law from the University of Paris in 1958.

Hassan Sadr began his career with Iran's Ministry of Justice serving as a prosecutor. He later transitioned to private law practice and quickly immersed himself in the national politics. For a brief period between 1941 and 1953, free press in Iran allowed him to launch a left-leaning daily journal, *Ghiam-e-Iran*, that soon attracted a relatively large number of loyal readers. He was one of the original founders of the National Front Movement that paved the way for the nationalization of Anglo-Iranian Oil Company in 1951. In 1952 when the United Kingdom filed a complaint against Iran's nationalization of its natural resources with the International Court of Justice, he prepared the response and personally presented the legal briefs to the Court in The Hague. His most important client was the prominent ex-prime minister, Dr. *Mossadegh*, accused by the Shah of committing treason in the aftermath of 1953 *coup d'état.*

PART I

Women's Rights: History and Evolution

PART II

Modern women's rights: Civil and
Moral Laws

Introduction

The topic

Morality and its application to western civil laws were of great interest in the 20th century in many societies. It was this topic and the relationship between defending and protecting women's rights and the health of a society, prescribed by Islam, that motivated Hassan Sadr to publish his "Women's Rights in Islam and Europe" in 1941

A timely publication

Women's Rights was published at a time when a significant segment of Iran's cultural and traditional values were under assault by the Shah's regime. 1940 Iran was politically and socially in a suppressed mode. Under the censorship of the press and a brutal watchdog on the pretext of intelligence service, people lived in an atmosphere of fear and despair throughout the country.

The purpose

In his book Hassan Sadr aimed to portray motherhood as a critical component of a family from the dawn of civilization. She would give birth to a child, nourish her child with her milk and blood, and nurture her children for many years after birth. The prime organizer of a family, he believed, would be the mother of the children as enforcer of "rules" and the stabilizer of the family validating the idea that well nurtured children would constitute a healthy family. Recognizing family as the first society, he concluded that only a healthy family can result in a healthy society, just and peaceful. Lastly, he considers reproduction the key purpose for family formation hence protecting women's rights will be a natural pre-requisite for such society.

The book provided a then-fresh perspective on old issues because opinions on moral issues were expressed by a legal expert, rather than by clerics. The endorsement of the book by religious leaders and legal scholars provided credibility. attracting intellectuals as well as the academia. The book became popular enough to be listed as students' "required reading" thanks to its well organized and engaging discussion of social issues. In particular the item-by-item explanation of the French Civil Code proved to be quite useful for the purpose of comparison.

The book was reprinted with new updates several times, the final in 1977.

Later works

After the 1953 Coup, Hassan Sadr frequently wrote articles on social issues for daily Iranian papers. He later attended school in France where he obtained his Doctorate from Paris University in 1958. He returned to his law practice in Iran and resumed his literary work. Two of his published books: "Ali, the Superhuman", 1959 which won the National Publishers Award provided a complete biography of the most important leader of Islam who also was instrumental in founding of Shia by his descendants. His other book "Algeria and the *Mojahedeen*", 1962 is a political commentary covering the struggle of the people of Algeria against colonialist France. The book appeared in the best seller list for many weeks.

PART I

Women's Rights: History and Evolution

In The Name of God All Encompassin**g**

Has Islam taught that men are superior to women?
And rights of woman are less that man in all levels?
Were the women of Early Islam removed from social and political affair?
Does God divide, from Islam perspective, his creatures into two distinct
groups of men and women?
Allowing one being at higher level, and another lower?

CHAPTER ONE
History and evolution of Roman law

The legal history of Rome covers three distinct periods: the Monarchy, the Republic and the Empire.

The Monarchy period began seven hundred years before Christ was born, lasting for more than three hundred years. The Republic was established in 364 BC and ended in 27 BC. The birth of the Roman Empire began with Augustine's coronation in the same year and ended with the death of Justinian, 565. The notable and significant period, from a legal point of view, began shortly before the end of the Republic and lasted through the end of the Empire's second century.

1. The Monarchy: During this period government structure comprised the king, who was either elected or had inherited the monarchy and a council known as the "Council of Elders". Additionally, the Senate usually was populated with heads of families who consulted and voted in any legislation and jointly administered the country's affairs with the king. Once in a while, and at the discretion of the king, another council

dred and fifty years later, membership to this council was opened to public.

2. **The Republic**[1] means an entity belonging to all. In this period, the executive branch was controlled by a "select" group of jurists and technocrats as government officials[2]. Top civil servant and military command were usually reserved for *Consuls*. *Questeures* were in charge of the country's finance and treasury and the public courts were assigned the task of protecting the interests of aristocrats and the wealthy families. *Edile Curule* were responsible for commerce and market affairs and *Preteurs Urbains* were in charge of more important functions such as final ruling on formal complaints between parties, enforceable by law. Their jurisdiction was limited to Roman citizens. Foreigners' complaints were referred to *Preteurs Peregrins*.

An important law written by a special committee *Desem Vir* and approved by the Republic is known as *La Laides Douze Tables*[3]. This has the significance of being the first book written as a code of law in 400 BC.

3. The Empire: L' Edit Principal

This period of history of Romans is the most important part of advancing the law which covers the first one- third of the entire period of the Empire. During this period, Roman law which up to then had only two sources, added a third source. The previous two sources were cultural tradition and legislated written laws. The discovery of the third source led to *L' Edit*[4].

The term for the judge to preside over a court was generally set as one year. Starting from the first day of his appointment he would be required to set certain rules and policies that he would enforce during his judgeship. This proclamation, known as *Edit*, had to be disseminated to the public and was enforced just like any other laws.

Collectively these policy statements constituted the basis for Roman jurisprudence. The roots of these policy statements were community habits and tradition. Since the new judge had familiarized himself with fundamentals and bases of his predecessor, he would overlook anything which was inconsistent with the existing practices of the community and simply ignore that in his written opinion.

Initially, the judge was not allowed to make decisions contrary to the governing laws. His duty was to follow and implement the letter of the law. Later on, he acquired the right to modify the law as he saw fit and in special cases and to incorporate any clarifications which were otherwise not foreseen by the law. Ultimately, judges extended and generalized their rights to modify and enhance the law as and when they deemed necessary.

Today's[5] law practices demonstrate that the Proclamations issued by judges differ little from official laws of the land, except the period during which it was enforced. Currently, research studies conducted on Roman laws are based on such jurisprudence because it contains the laws and rules harmonious with the generally held beliefs and practices of people.

The first two centuries of the Empire constituted the most significant period for Roman laws and judicial systems to flourish. The legal institutions showed a remarkable accomplishment and advancement so much that it is reflected in today's general thinking of legal scholars (mostly, private branches of civil law) in most European countries. The most notable scholars of Roman law in this period were *Gaius*, who authored "Gaius Principles", *Paul Ulpien* author of "Rules of Law", *Modest-in* and *Papinien*. For complex cases, judges applied these individuals references and opinions for ruling. In the event a majority of votes among the panel judges was not reached, *Papinien*[6] opinion would prevail.

The period of the Roman Empire, beginning with Emperor *Augustus* and extending to Emperor *Diuclessien*, is known as *Dyarchie* period (dual imperial government). The power and the governing body were represented by the Emperor and the Senate. The States were divided in two groups: some governed by the Emperor and some by the Senate. In order to maintain the dual government regime each State was self-governed.

After the reign of *Diuclessien* had ended and until the dissolution of the Empire, the government adopted a single authority with *reliable source*, all entrusted to *the Emperor* himself[7]. Gradually, Proclamations of judges became less important and were limited to specific issues because the Emperor himself was the First judge of the Empire and could overturn all judges declarations. The Emperor could issue four types of Proclamations: *L. Edit, Mandat, Decret* and *Rescrit.* The Emperor's *Edit* was similar to judges Proclamation previously explained with one exception that it could not be annulled unless the Emperor chose to do so; it remained legally binding even after the Emperor's death due to the hereditary nature of the new Empire. Additionally, since the Emperor was the head of the legislative body his Proclamation would be interpreted as superior to all others including judges' Proclamations which were sometime against the existing laws. *Manda* were Directives issued by the Emperor to ruling government officials of States and regions outlining the manner of handling defeated nations and occupied countries. *Decret* was reserved for cases that the Emperor, because of his jurisdiction, would intervene in a dispute between two parties and would issue a ruling based on a new principle which had no precedent. *Rescrit* occurred when the two parties of complaint or dispute chose to accept the Emperor's arbitration in lieu of prosecution. The opinion expressed by the Emperor due to his jurisdiction would then be noted as the law.

Towards the end of 4th century, Romans began compiling all rules of the law belonging to any of the categories mentioned above, all in a single document. In early 5th century Emperor *Theodosius* II, arranged a book of law known as *Code Theodose.* It contained all rulings, opinions expressed by both judges and counsellor in various cases as well as the jurisprudence of past emperors covering the period of 312-438, making it an official status of the law. This *Code,* however, did not annul the contradictory laws of the past.

The last Roman period of evolution of law was during the reign of the famed Emperor Justinian (527-565) who contributed a series of important legal works. The most notable one was "*Code Justinian*", a collection of legal works "*Novelle*", "*Institutes*" and "*Digeste*". *Code Justinian* covers all the legal works from 1st to 4th century. *Institutes* provides the laws during his reign particularly of value for students of law school and *Digeste*, the most comprehensive book of civil laws and judicial systems. It contains 50 sections, each divided in several chapters, each consisting of several parts. In this book, *Justinian* describes the thoughts and opinions of famous lawyers of the past centuries especially the five notable individuals mentioned before.

Furthermore, since his (*Justinian*) period had witnessed the evolution and perfection, causing fundamental changes in the law, he reviewed the rulings of older cases making appropriate modifications which would then allow the book to be comprehensive both from legal and historical point of view.

CHAPTER TWO
Role of religion and family in ancient Rome

The foundation and organization of ancient Rome were based on religious beliefs. The significance of family, *Pater Familias* and father's extraordinary power resulted from the importance as well as the influence of religion[1]. Religion in ancient Rome was an internal and private affair; that is, each family had its own specific "gods" unknown to other families, who were then considered "unbelievers". Accordingly, the Romans concept of religion had two characteristics. First, they practiced Polytheism. Second, each family worshipped private gods. Each family worshiped his ancestors and every father was human until he died at which time he would join the rank of gods qualified to be worshiped by the survivors. Since each family worshiped its own gods,[2] anyone from the same family mistakenly, or otherwise, who worshiped gods of another family would be an infidel.

The father was the head and indisputable ruler of the family. His leadership originated from his religious faithfulness which was the root of his extraordinary and unchallenged influence in the family because religion was the foundation of the Roman family. Family members, namely, sons, daughters and mother were so obedient to the father that determining their affairs and their fate, including life and death, were all in his hands. He alone, for instance, would decide the newly born child's fate. A child's life would be terminated If the father did not accept the new born. For example, if the child was born as illegitimate, or of a non-Roman foreign father, in which case retaining the child would be considered disrespectful towards his gods. The father had also the right to end the life of each family member especially his wife and at any event he would not be obligated to report and explain his reasoning to any legal authorities.

Family members

The family comprised a wife, sons and daughters at any age except those sons who had been "freed" by the command of the father, and daughters who were married and hence members of another family. Two other members were also included: slaves, freed slaves by the head of family under certain conditions and those serving the master in a limited way outside the residency of the family. By freeing the slave the head of family was entitled to impose any conditions that he felt would be beneficial to him. Free[3] was a person who was free throughout his life and remained free; whereas freed[4] was someone who had been a slave for certain period and subsequently granted freedom. The son of a freed slave was free.

Legal proximity and natural relationship

A noteworthy observation in Roman families was that proximity or relationship, whether customary or legally[5], only existed between man and man. No legal relationship between man and woman or woman and woman existed, except merely as type of natural blood relationship[6]. Two individuals could have legal as well as natural relationship such as two family brothers while under the control of their father. They could, otherwise, only have legal relationship such as adopted son of someone's biological son. It was also possible that they would have natural relationship without (the existence of) any legal proximity between them. The example for this would be the relation between two brothers-one being under the control of the father of the family while the other brother, free and of his own legal standing. Other examples include relationships between brothers and sisters, two sisters and mother and daughter.

Legal proximity was a means for linking family sons who lived under the control of their one father[7]. As such there was no proximity relationship between daughter and father, daughter and mother, sister and brother, son and mother and husband and wife. This also applied to two brothers, one of whom was freed or evicted from the family. On the contrary, there was a legal relationship between brothers who were not presently under the control of one father (deceased father). Based on the foregoing, one can conclude that the origin of family formation and its members relationships, was based on religion. Legal relationship was seen as its pronounced effect on the subject of inheritance. The only heirs of the deceased were his legal relatives. The heirs of father's assets were only those sons who were his legal sons. Neither the daughters, nor the sons who were freed or expelled, nor the wife would be entitled to any portion of his inheritance. On the other hand, the adopted son would be entitled to the same inheritance as legal sons. Historical evolution of Roman legal frame led to a gradual decrease in the significance of legal proximity. At the same time, the natural and real relationship was strengthened. At last, the natural relationship replaced the artificial proximity relationship towards the demise of the Empire.

Freedom and attributes of sons

As mentioned elsewhere, daughters and wives did not possess any legal personality in ancient Rome. The son was also not a legal person and lacked legal rights and legal transaction authority as long as the father was alive. The day that the father died, however, the elder son would become the father of family, thereby possessing all the power that his father had.

Other sons could form separate families and remain in the same family under the authority of the new father. The choice of leaving or staying was conditional on not being a minor. The age of puberty was determined to be twelve for female and fourteen for male, divided into two periods of seven years. Later on, the age limits gradually were raised up to twenty five years.

It was also possible that the living father would grant his sons freedom and legal personality. Freedom was either absolute, or relative. Absolute implied complete freedom from the father's protection by already forming a family of his own. He would live and work and would be empowered by legal and civil rights. Naturally, in this case his wife would also be free from domination of her husband's father. The relative freedom initially did not have legal acceptance and it was unofficially derived from ceremonies and traditions; it gradually was expanded sufficiently to be used as a legal tool.

Notwithstanding the basic premise of denying any financial ownership to the family sons, the father if assured of his son's business astuteness, may have provided him with a small amount of capital[8] for starting a business resulting in modest savings. Later on, it was resolved that the spoils[9] of wars fought by family sons would not be distributed among family fathers; instead the actual owners, that is the sons, would have full possession over that. Later yet, it was resolved that the sons who were employed by the government or the Church would also own and control their earnings[10]. Additionally, in the event the relatives on the mother's side or a son with no sons, had left any inheritance, the son(s) would be the heir and actual owner of the inheritance.[11] However, administering of its proceeds would be the special right of the father.

All freedom related matters of family sons, whether absolute or relative and would apply equally to adopted sons. This allowed a son, who would never be free in his own family before the passing of his father, to be adopted by another family by seeking and actively promoting himself to become a member of a new family. He would then be liberated from his (biological) father's influence and the worshiping of his family gods, achieving absolute or relative freedom with the concurrence of the new family father.

A noteworthy point in family switching was that it could be extended to a family father. He could enter an agreement with another family to strip himself from his legal personality and accept the authority of another family's father due to social or financial reasons. In this case all members of his family would also become the subjects of the new family's father. This family transformation essentially eliminated one family's legal personality and some of the family's gods which, in turn, would require social and religious pomp and circumstance, pending the special committee's *(Comis Par Cries)* permission. Such transactions were therefore rarely permitted.

CHAPTER THREE
Status of woman in Roman family and marriage

In ancient Rome, woman was treated as a daughter by the father, or her husband's father. Therefore, if her husband was the head of the family she was considered a sister to her own children and in accordance with Roman religious jurists: wedding for a young woman is like another "birth of a new born". She would also become a daughter to her husband[1]. The living father of her husband would consider this "new born" daughter the same as her husband's sister, that is, his own daughter.

As it was pointed out in the previous chapter all members of the family especially the wife and daughters would possess no legal personality nor any power. The young sons after either being freed by family head or upon the death of the father would become independent and the most senior son would be elected as the family head. Contrary to the sons, who even during their dependency and under supervision were not seriously mistreated by the father, the daughters and wives were subjected to various kinds of transactions as if they were objects. A wife and or daughter did not have the right of ownership, associations and intermingling with anyone outside of their family; in short, they had no control over their own lives. The father at anytime and at his discretion could sell them, loan them, or rent them and or kill them.

Plainly, if the wife is denied her title as a social person, she will be naturally deprived of human rights and every legal protection such as inheritance. Furthermore she will not be allowed to express any opinions in family affairs. Even after the mother's son replaces his father and becomes a new head of the family, her status remains the same. This is not surprising since from a legal as well as social point of view there is basically no relationship between son and mother. A son who becomes the head of the family does not recognize his mother and his sisters as legal relatives. They only maintain a natural relationship as an extension of blood relation, or blood-sameness.

Marriage in Rome

The laws of Rome recognize two types of marriage: "official" and "unofficial" marriage. The latter would have no legal bearing and therefore no religious basis. Such a marriage contract between the parties would be considered null and void. The family father would do his best to prevent this sort of marriage which is merely because the couple show a desire to get married . More important, without a religious ceremony such marriage is considered meaningless. His so's new wife (his daughter) would not be allowed to learn, under any circumstances, the secrets of the her (father) family's religion while worshipping the private gods of her husband. In the event such a marriage leads to the birth of a child, the family father would not consider the child fit or acceptable to join the family for the purpose of family continuity and would condemn the child to death.

The "official" marriage was generally conducted in any of the following manner.

1. Transfer of bride from her father's quarters to that of her husband, known as Manus.

Under this arrangement the bride exits from her father's domain of influence and joins the circle of followers of her husband's family. The head of the (new) family would be either her husband or her husband's father. This method of marriage would then require special ceremonial arrangement and particular rules to ensure that the transfer has properly taken place. First, the bride's father as well as bridegroom's father – and in the event of his death the bridegroom himself- would appear in the chamber of a judge or special judges. Then prayers are performed and recitals and songs are conducted whereupon the bride would instantly give up her family religion and as a result, from then on, she would only be obedient to the head of new family and worships that family's gods.

2. Transfer of rights and paternal authority, known as Coemcylo.

Here a special transaction would take place between bride's father and husband or husband's father as the parties of transaction and the bride would become the "object" of the transaction. In such a transaction the bride's father would transfer all rights and paternal authority that he possessed over her daughter to the husband or the husband's father. This transfer might be free of any compensation or against receipt of funds in the manner of a sale. The important differentiation between these two methods (1) and (2) is that in method (2) the bride would not have been transferred from her paternal home to her husband's family; therefore no change of religion would have taken place and as such she would not be under the control of the head of new family. This situation which appears to be contrary to the basic premise of legitimate marriage became the acceptable norm for Romans from the time that social evolution and legal advances gradually reduced the influence of religion. It reduced the influence of the head of a family which, in turn, lessened the importance of family title.

3. The "possession and statute of limitation[2]"
is a manner in which a man possesses a woman by taking her to his
home under a pretext. Following cohabitation and her living at his quarters for at least one year, the woman would then be considered his "official" wife. The arrangement is considered interrupted if the woman can
avoid cohabitation for at least three consecutive nights. In this case the
statute of limitation would no longer apply and the man could no longer
have any claim (of ownership) over her.

It goes without saying that in the above case, and given the general status of woman with total lack of respect for her in the society, the opinion of a woman played no part in her choosing a husband. She would
be forced to submit unconditionally to any decision that her father or
guardian would make.

This weakness and humiliation was not just applied to young daughters and women, in which case one could attribute the act of possession
to youth and lack of experience of young women; hopefully, at some
point, they would mentally and socially be able to overcome that. The
disturbing issue, however, was that the underlying treatment of women
as a non person during their entire life in every phase of life, including
married life. They were systematically denied rights of legal transaction
and even private affairs of their household. The women were simply not
considered capable or qualified for anything.

Such unfairness and illogical assessment were observed at all levels of
Romans legal rights. As an example, a debtor who had failed to pay
his debt was liable to be taken as "prisoner" by the creditor who was
able to secure an enforceable ruling such as final judgement from the
courthouse, especially convened for this purpose[3]. In such a case the
creditor could proceed through a special executive legal body[4] where
the assumption was made that the legal relation of giving and taking
between the persons of both creditor and debtor implied that creditor
had the right to take the debtor, who had failed to pay his debt, to his

home and to imprison him in chains. If within sixty days no one had offered the payment on behalf of the debtor, the creditor had the right to sell his prisoner as slave to recover his debt.

Nowadays, of course, imprisonment on the basis of civil complaints does not exist, except in case of the government as creditor; further, it is only applicable to criminal cases.

CHAPTER FOUR
Religion, family and marriage
in ancient Greece

The famed Greek civilization, this intellectual leaven of ingenuity of man, has been built on top of the ruins of barbarism and savagery of ignorant tribes of ancient Greek. Religion in Greece, as in ancient Rome, was an internal and private affair and, similar to Rome, each family worshipped the spirit of its ancestors. Every morning and evening the family members gathered around the family's sacred fire-temple and by reciting special prayers dedicated food and drinks to the fire, while worshipping portraits and impressions of their fathers which were arranged all around the fireplace. Each family had a private cemetery for family members within the farm adjacent to the family residence. Other features of religious practices equally resembled those of ancient Rome, already discussed.

Family
The family's inception, continuity and observance of religious duties as well as the sovereignty of the head of the family are all derived from

the strength of religious leadership. The basis of founding a family was never dependent on personal desire nor from sentimental feelings. On the contrary, worshiping of the ancestors would make one family distinct from another. Marriage was considered a religious and sacred affair because the husband would allow a woman from outside of his family, to learn about his family's private religious secrets and to worship family's special gods. Not surprisingly, wedding ceremonies took place only in presence of family's gods, which was totally unrelated to public gods such as Jupiter.

The necessity of maintaining family's continuity, and hence the indispensability of marriage and prohibition of unmarried life, were devised to allow the family successors to serve food and drinks to family's ancestors through the family fire-temple. This enabled them to survive as gods; otherwise, they would be downgraded to the level of wretched people.

Form this point of view, marriage and reproduction were expected from the youth. The *Licorgue* laws prohibit unmarried status and set penalties for those who break the law. Since the intent of marrying is to reproduce male offspring for family there was no objection to divorcing a woman who was barren or unable to produce a son. Historian *Herodotus*, names two Spartan kings divorcing their sterile wives. In Greece (and India) if sterility was caused by the man, his brother or nearest of kin would be allowed to impregnate the woman in which case the children would be considered those of the real husband. Bearing a daughter had no effect in reproduction because she would leave her father's fire-temple and would practice the religion of her husband's family and the continuity of the new family was only made possible by the male children. To counter this deficiency, adoption did exist in its true sense, with official legal proximity already in place, between any pair of male children. It was reserved for those without son and or any tribes, in most civilized places like Rome, Greece, India, Iran and Arabia where survival was considered dependent on having male children. Pluto and *Plutocrats*[1], state that official legal proximity between male individuals exists if they practice a common religion and worship the same god. Or, if two persons reach certain limit of commonality in worshipping a god they possess a legal proximity to each other.

Marriage

According to existing narratives, there were no marriage contracts in ancient Greece and the Greeks lived absolutely as mixed people before the *Cencops* period of 1700BC. Children only knew their mothers and their surname was the same as their mothers' since it was difficult to identify their father. Although this sounds like a fable, but the existence of free intercourse in lieu of marriage is documented in certain parts of the world (and even now among some primitive tribes in Africa and South Pacific islands). Further more, the recently published works of Greek and non Greek writers confirm the truthfulness of this social phenomenon. Later, gradual social changes resulted in official religious marriage, as an alternative choice to counter the free intercourse, which ultimately became the norm and a publicly adopted practice. The religious marriage ceremonies consisted of three parts:

First: The ceremonial affairs were conducted at family's fire-temple where the father transfered his rights to his daughter, or effectively to her husband, in exchange for cash or gift. The gift could be in the form of special service which the husband could volunteer such as free labor.

Second: Wedding ceremonies that would take place during the passage of bride and bridegroom, journeying from her family home to the couple's new quarters with public viewing of the parade. Here, the bride with her all-white dress, and representing a religious event, would be seated in a push-cart wearing a garland. The designated priests (Soothsayers) carrying torch would sing a hymn-which later became part of all rituals of the wedding. Inside her husband's quarters, the bride would pretend that she is not inclined to enter her husband's home and must feign that she is being abducted and forced to enter the new home.

She would then pretend that she is taken against her will by screaming and asking for help from her entourage. At last the bridegroom succeeds in abducting and forcibly take her into his home.

A routine research on the subject of ancient civilizations makes it evident that the tradition of abduction is rooted in proof of manhood, hence bridegroom's daring capability. In other words, a young man is capable to be a bridegroom only if he is able to fight with bride's family and against their wishes by abducting their daughter. Among some backward tribes this struggle in the fashion of abducting still exists in a true sense of the word and is still being practiced.

Third: This stage of marriage ceremony takes place inside the husband's home and in presence of all family members in front of family's sacred fire-temple. Here, the couple would make the offering and perform specified recitals.

Some remnant of forced and possessive marriage existed in Spartan society for a long time and usually the families did not marry their daughters before they were ripe and ready to bear a child.

Polygamy was apparently not practiced by Greeks and Romans. Men did not have more than one wife, but every man in accordance to his financial means would keep a number of lovers within his family residence. The children born by these women were treated, legally, socially and individually the same as the ones born by the official wife. The mother of Ulysses[2] was the king's lover. In Greece a woman had no legal or social property and her husband could loan her or donate her to his friends. Father of *Demosthenes* donated his mother to one of his friends. *Licorgue*, the famous Legislator had recommended loaning the wife, albeit to good and capable men who are able to deliver good children. An elder man was obligated to find a young man for his young wife provided that the young man was pious. Plato and Socrates also followed teachings of this philosophy. Socrates lent his friend's wife

Xantippe to *Alcibiade*, the Orator, another friend. A treacherous wife who had an illegitimate relationship with a strange man, if caught in the act could be murdered by the husband.

Divorce
Both marriage and divorce were executed by the guardian of the daughter, initially without her prior knowledge, but gradually this extraordinary power of the guardianship of daughters were reduced. Divorce was basically allowed in Greece and Rome, but its occurrence was rare for a long time and not that easy. The procedure was that woman and her husband along with members of both families would gather by the husband's family fire-temple, exchanging angry words. After a while with complete silence, observed by both fathers, divorce was consummated.

Woman's inheritance
The basic premise has been the denial of inheritance, but later on sympathetic feelings led to exploring special ways for women to share the inheritance. For example, daughter could marry his father's son as inheritor provided they did not have the same mother. Another way was to adopt a son and marry family's daughter to him who would then be the inheritor. It was possible that the deceased, in his will, would order his heir to marry his daughter. Since in practice man and wife shared the family wealth, the family daughter would ultimately benefit from her father's inheritance.

On occasions, a man with one female child could marry her to a man and would make an agreement with him that his intent is to produce a son who would then follow his mother's ancestral religion in which case the son-to-be would be son of his grand father.

As the woman's basic rights evolved the issue of female child inheritance improved somewhat. Daughter(s), in absence of son, were allowed to share the inheritance, but in that case she had to marry her father's relative who would be an heir in case of the deceased having no daughters.

If the daughter was already married, she had to cancel her marriage contract and as an unmarried woman she was able to re-marry to his father's relative.

It is noteworthy that in general inheritance in Greece and also India was indivisible, and since the senior son would be the head and guardian of family's religion, he would inherit the real estates and other illiquid assets; sometime the entire inheritance. Even though during the time of *Demosthenes* this practice was negated, the residence of the deceased would still belong to senior[3] son. A famous Greek saying notes: "The eldest son is the religious son while the others are born of love". Although the heir and legal owner are senior sons, different methods are adopted to assist the other sons who may be otherwise denied their share of inheritance.

The conclusion can be drawn from study of woman's status and the opportunity in the ancient civilizations of Greek and Rome, that in the beginning woman was an object for being owned and later a tool for reproduction as well as satisfying man's lust and passion. Under no circumstances was she considered a partner in man's life. She was simply not considered a possessor of *all* human faculties. A majority of thinkers (of the time) believed that woman did not possess an eternal soul and therefore had no right to live after her husband's death. The practice of burning of woman, alive along with the dead body of her husband in India and other parts of the world stemmed from this belief.

At any event, the wrenching situation for woman continued for centuries until Christ was born. The religious thinking and teaching of Christ and his followers encouraged the legislators and knowledgeable leaders to end or modify the inhuman treatment of women. In the East, with the advent of the Prophet of Islam and his subsequent teachings the society was completely transformed resulting in emancipation of women, the endowment of freedom and the right of an individual to live free. In the West, woman's social standing improved incrementally from the position of an object of being owned [4] to "a person who has the right to own" and they were gradually given social rights[5] at much slower pace.

After societies' recognition and acceptance of woman as a person with social standing, the attention of legislators and thinkers of Eastern and Western societies was directed towards investigating different schools of thought regarding woman's faculties. The issues were whether the woman, from the point of view of creation and the faculty of mind as it appeared, was weaker and less able and hence should have been given lesser rights, or whether this backwardness was the consequence of thousands of years of neglect and lack of attention to proper training and education that may have caused backwardness. By paying more attention to proper nurturing, women would have been considered as collaborators and wives of men at all positions of social, political and economic aspects of society and hence the beneficiary of all rights. In later chapters these opinions and their effects of a women's rights in various countries are reviewed and discussed.

In the past three centuries[6] proponents of complete equality of man and woman have made serious efforts, and to a certain extent have succeeded, towards achieving that goal. From one century to the next the sphere of women's rights has expanded, particularly in the West. For example in the Scandinavian countries daughters were excluded from inheritance. They only received a nominal amount as the dowry for their marriage from the person[7] whose permission was required for marriage to take place. In 1262, daughters were entitled to one third(1/3) of inheritance and by 1871 there was full equality between sons and daughters. In France, groups for support of women's rights[8] are organized, comprising the promotors as well as social and legal authorities who have made serious efforts to influence French parliament's legislations, with some degree of success.

CHAPTER FIVE
Social organizations in Iran before Islam

Government by class distinction

Prior to Islam, the system of government, in ancient Iran, was similar to ancient Rome. These societies, based on a multi socio-economic classes, were strictly segregated and, each class maintained its own designated position of privileges. Contrary to democratic societies, prestige of a person represented his roots, his sect or race and his "belonging" to that privileged group. Such group designation ignored any personal capabilities and qualifications of its members.

Islam rejected this classification in 7th century by introducing laws based on justice and freedom of mankind embracing a vast part of the eastern civilization. The 18th century French Revolution was precisely about rejection of such classification which was still enforced in western societies. By then the significance of origin or the lineage or class privilege, *per se*, was no longer the acceptable criteria for distinction. The personal capability and performance as well as the virtues of moral values and knowledge became the new measuring instruments for evaluating a person's merit. *Salman -e- Farsi*, an unknown Persian with no material belongings, was recognized by Islam, as a preferred person of faith, to *Abdol- Rahman- Ouf,* a wealthy Arab. The French Revolution with its Human Rights Declaration[1] made it possible for every capable French citizen, who was of sound mind to achieve the highest position in public and private sector.

Social organizations

The reserved distinction, based on social standing, remained intact during the entire period of dynasties of ancient Iran prior to Islam; although the types of social levels somewhat varied in *Achaemenid, Arsacid* (also known as Parthian) and *Sassanid*. For instance, the Achaemenid started off with three distinct groups, namely, divine, military and farmers who was mostly peasants. Later on a group, known as, artisans were added during Sassanid dynasty. The original Iranians of the Aryan race, only concentrated on the first three professions and considered artisan and trade as a low level profession reserved for non-Iranians.

Sassanid organizations

The new organization during Sassanid reign was made up of four groups, with one exception, of combining artisans and farmers as part of the fourth group, making room for a new class of educators and government bureaucrats:

- Spirituals

- Military

- Educators and government employees

- Masses which included farmers, artisans, traders and speculators and any other entrepreneurs.

The foundation and support of Iranian social fabric, aside from property ownership, was based on race and relation[2]. The nobles and aristocrats were shielded from the masses by having special privileges. Each class lived under a set of rigid and traditional rules which never changed. One such social rule forbade seeking a higher rank, which would be above the person's existing one, within the group classification.

The tasks of protecting the wealth and properties as well as the purity of blood, race and inter-family relation were particularly the responsibility of the law enforcement[3]. Other important tasks were recording, filing and archiving documents with government body and prohibiting the public from acquisition of aristocrats' properties. No one from the four designated classes was allowed to move from a lower class to the upper level. No individual whether capable, qualified, or impressively rich would be permitted to change his class status to which he was assigned.

Also, within the mass population no one could be engaged in a profession without his ancestral background in the same field which implied he was not meant to execute that particular task. The rationale was that if a person was to be engaged in a business, unaware of its secrets he may ruin the job that he had undertaken and as a result an expected well-executed social affair will be hampered. The kings would never allow low level people to engage in royal affairs.

Ferdowsi in his Epic story of *Shahnameh* describes the war that King *Noshiravan* waged against Romans. He needed to raise three hundred thousand Dinars for financing the war. He dispatched an agent to find a wealthy trader or farmer, willing to loan him the money. The agent found a shoe maker who would willingly offer the money and, in return, asked for king's permission that his capable and smart son be given an opportunity, as special case, to be trained by educators in order to prepare him for becoming a teacher. The agent took the money and relayed the message via *Bouzarjomehr*; whereupon the king ordered the money to be returned promptly.

This story shows the evidence that extreme caution was exercised in protecting the established class boundaries which under no circumstances was it wise for a person from the fourth class to acquire the learning of knowledge and skills of upper level who would then be considered a member of that class. As such he would take away the inherited job from intellectuals and teachers. Further, his lack of origin and genealogy would be an impediment in utilizing his knowledge with sincerity and to serve the well being of society.

Occasionally, however, upon performing special ceremonies this elevation of class was possible. For example a person being at the level of genius and showing extraordinary capability and art skill who would be methodically and strictly trained by religious leaders and of designated class to certify and report his citizenship to the king at which time with the king's blessing he would join the higher class. At any event and prior to promotion, he must be fully trained and his qualification must be certified.

Merit and deficiency of ruling by class

The advantage of this kind of governing is that anyone within his own domain of expertise, screened and skilled from noble birth and noble blood, would lead the authorities in social affairs to good and sound policies.

It has, however, two important shortcomings. For one thing, a capable person of lower classes with God given artistic talent and an ingenious mind may be left behind and wasted. Another drawback is that if the successor is a mean person, by nature, and is born wicked his immorality will corrupt the social fabric of the society.

To compensate for the latter deficiency, the Sassanid government made every efforts by employing the best methods of teaching and training of people of upper level that it would have been inconceivable for members of such elite family to be depraved. Their physical, intellectual and moral faculties were trained in best possible manner, but the extraordinary privileges of upper classes and the inaccessibility of proper education and training facilities for masses as well as the villagers poor standard of living had made the social and health conditions of the average people so vulnerable and morally bankrupt that even with an impressive military strength the nation was unable to repel Arabs aggression and the government of Sassanid eventually fell.

Democratic governing bodies, on the other hand, measure the development and maturity by setting criteria such as moral excellence, virtue and skill. Teaching of Islam, while respecting ownership in principle, has rejected the basis of social classes. The ambassador of Islam's army meeting with king of Egypt *Maghoume*s was a black man. When he arrived the king demanded that the black man be removed from his sight. They told *Amr-va'as*, the army commander, to assign another person. He replied that would be impossible because this black man is more virtuous, braver and more magnanimous than all of us and no one is more qualified than he who can represent us. Many centuries later, one of the articles of Human Rights in 1789 French Revolution, states: "Everyone is entitled to strive for any job or position for which he is qualified".

To summarize, class privileges of one over another had been an established principle in ancient Iran. To protect the status of race and to prevent mixing of corrupt blood of low class person with that of nobility no man from the lower class was allowed to marry a woman of the upper class because such marriage of unequals would have resulted in creating and reproducing of ignoble, causing the decline and deterioration of families in the future.

CHAPTER SIX
Status of woman in Iran before Islam

There are two important considerations that should not be overlooked with regards to legal status and social position of woman in ancient Iran.

1. It is generally known that the overall status of woman from the inception of tribes and social gatherings has progressively improved as one goes back in time, starting from very dark days of misery that women have endured. Historically, three distinct periods can be identified where the laws for protecting the rights of woman have evolved throughout the world:

First Period: The period of savagery, ignorance and paganism- During this time woman was not considered a human being at all and she was treated with extreme harshness and hardship. Woman was an object of ownership and was counted in the rank of slaves and four legged animals for load carrying purpose. As a result they lacked any legal personality and authority. A man could have sold his wife, loaned her, rented her, donated her or killed her. With the slightest excuse the wife would be the rightful recipient of the harshest punishment. Often she was tied to the trunk of a tree and whipped. On the other hand, she was responsible for the most difficult chores and the heaviest tasks. The only option, that she thought for herself, would be to commit suicide. The remnants of this period in Africa and indigenous part of Americas and South Pacific islands still exist[1].

Second Period: This period which witnessed the flourishing of civilization in Greece, Egypt, Rome and Iran, was influenced by the advent of monotheistic religions teaching as well as important contributions of reformers of the time. Human feelings and sentiments were promoted and integrated into reason and knowledge[2]. During this period woman materially and individually qualified for the title of a human being, but only to the extent of being a partner in sharing man's life. Still, she was not considered a human being either intellectually or socially. She still lacked any legal personality, was controlled by her husband and was completely obedient to his thought and his will.

Third Period: As will be discussed later, Islam with its superior teachings, in addition to saving woman from her injustice and deplorable situation, established a legal personality for woman for the first time. The continuation of this social upheaval eventually reached western societies, manifested in a series of civil laws leading to the present. Woman's demands for full equality with men are now mostly realized and women enjoy all the available social benefits.

2. The existence of privileged classes in Iran before Islam resulted in a vastly different kind of woman's legal personality and social privileges, which was generally divided into two types: The women of nobility and those of "all other classes".

Iranian women during the second period were affected by historical changes. Yet, it could categorically be stated that they had no social personality or qualification to enter into a legal contract and the man's decision or vote would have been the influencing factor. Although the spirit of privileged class gives the apparent impression that their confinement or otherwise their freedom was not the same between the privileged and "all other" classes, in reality the woman of the blue blooded class had the same position with respect to man as their counterparts in lower class. In either class the women were not entitled to any opinion, nor had any control over their own lives, nor the ability to recognize good from bad. In both classes the man's dominance and absolute rule were visible and unbearable. Indeed, the only difference between these two classes of women was manifested in material livelihood and the comfort and convenience as well as the quality of their enjoyment. Enjoyment itself, however, is measured relative to expectation, sociability and human habits with respect to senses. All things considered, it may be concluded that both classes had equal shares in comfort and toil.

Marriage

As the existing documents show, polygamy in ancient Iran had been allowed, usually devised for convenience of men who were wealthy and could afford the extra expenses. Accordingly, the poor men only chose one wife, while a wealthy man could have had several wives. Only one among them was, however, considered the authentic wife and man's partner for life, known as *Shah-zan*. The rest of the wives were mostly procured slaves and prisoners of war who lived and worked as servants in the family residence. A man could apparently have had more than one *Shah-zan*, in which case every one of them would be provided with separate and independent living quarters and the husband was required to maintain their subsistence for the rest of her life. The welfare of *Shah-zan*'s children was also the husband's responsibility until such time that they formed their own family. As for the servants, only their sons would qualify to live in the family quarters. The fate of daughters after being born remained unknown.

The daughter could not express any opinion, assent or dissent, in selecting her husband. Rather she had to obey her father's judgement which was legally his right. She could only refuse to accept the chosen husband requesting another choice be made by her father.

Any moral training and religious teaching of daughter were the responsibility of mother who was also given the right of selecting husband for her in case the father was deceased. If mother was also deceased the responsibility would be transferred to the nearest kin.

Daughters were required to be married as soon as they had reached puberty, in order not to have impeded the reproduction process. The father, at the time of marrying her daughter, would transfer to her husband all of his rights exercised on her daughter as well as all of his duties to her. In return for this transaction the father would receive a gift in the form of cash or property, but if upon consummating the marriage it became evident that there is a fault with his daughter such as sterility, the husband could then retrieve the gift and divorce his wife.

Marriage: Immediate family member (incestuous)

As mentioned elsewhere, protection of Iranian family's relations from defiling and contamination was the biggest and firmest pillar that ancient Iranian society had heavily leaned on and as a result, marrying to outsiders was prohibited. The degree of keeping this principle intact, was so extreme that in some cases anyone outside the family was considered an alien. In this manner not only one was not allowed to marry a non-Iranian, nor was marrying a person from lower class possible. The inter-class marriage was also prohibited. The assumption was that per chance one's blood circulation other than the inherited blood of family member might cause blood corruption, in which case, the decline of family's morality would be an abomination.

Most families arranged for intermarriage of male and female within the same family, where incest was allowed. Marriage between brother and sister by *Farr-Izadi*[3] would light up and drive away Davian. Not only this subject was well documented in Sassanid literature at the time, but there are historical references to support it. For example, marrying of *Bahraam Chubineh* and his sister *Gerdieh* and marriage of *Mehran Gashnasb* with his sister before her conversion to Christianity. In conclusion, the criterion for committing incest was to protect the blood relation to which a complete attention was certainly[4] accorded in the social setting of that period.

Ideal marriage

Among various types of marriage in ancient Iran there was, according to contents of a *Tenser*'s letter, a special type of "ideal"marriage designed to ensure the continuity of reproduction. If a husband had died without any surviving son then the surviving wife would be obliged to marry the nearest male relative of her deceased husband. If for any reason the deceased had no wife his daughter or the nearest of his female relative would be obliged to marry the nearest of male relative. If there was no female relative the family would procure the necessary dowry for a woman, using the husband's personal wealth, and marry her to a relative of the deceased husband. The son resulting from this marriage would be considered the deceased husband's replacement. An indolent or lazy individual who failed his responsibility in executing this task would be as if he had murdered a population because the line of succession needed for continuity of the deceased family generation had been broken and the family's lifeline of the deceased had been lost[5].

Such beliefs were common among nations of ancient civilizations such as Greece, Rome, India and Egypt, whose criterion and basis were uniquely associated with existence of classes and their survival of families as the important pillar of their nation's backbone. The worthy children were the male ones. The female children had no value because they would leave father's domain and further, no inheritance would be shared with them in order to prevent dilution of family wealth.

In ancient Greece, Rome and India, as mentioned before, the ancestors had the status of god and continuity of such heavenly status was
contingent on survival of their male children in order to receive food
from them through the family's Fire-temple; otherwise, and in absence
of food, the ancestors would fall from godly status to wretched persons.
Therefore, families must have always remained committed to insist on
having male children. Having or not having female children was considered to be irrelevant. From this view, divorcing a wife who was barren
or unable to produce a son for a long spell had not been objectionable.

Adoption was a natural substitute to offset this deficiency which existed
in ancient civilizations, namely, Iran, Rome and Greece whereby
adopted son would replace real son. He would benefit from all legal
rights that were otherwise available to a real son because he could keep
the family's sacred flame of family's fire-temple lighted. In this manner
the name of the deceased would be kept alive.

In ancient Iran, *Shah-zan* could have been given the title of an adopted
son and manage the entire inheritance of her deceased husband, but
the other wives, the servants were not accorded the same privileges.
A *Shah-zan* who assumed the responsibility of adopted son could not
remarry. Neither was she permitted to contemplate or prepare herself
for doing so. She had to ethically remain virtuous and not engaged in
the same situation with another family. A man, however, was accepted
as adopted son in several families.

Woman's inheritance

As *shah-zan* in the title role of adopted son could replace a son, she was
also entitled to inheritance as a son, but unmarried daughters would
obtain one half of son's share. A married daughter had no right to inheritance because she belonged to another family and was to remain there
for the rest of her life. The servants male or female had no rights to the
inheritance, but the father, usually as a gift, would give something to
them either as living will or after his death. In a will, similar to present

law practices in civilized world, the deceased was not allowed to donate all or any portion of his inheritance to anyone outside of the family, depriving legal inheritors, except in special cases and only under certain conditions. At any event, the "unmarried" daughters, would receive each one share while *Shah-Zan* would receive two shares.

The criterion for this denial (to unmarried daughter) is the influence of "blood relation" applied everywhere in distribution of inheritance, which will be discussed in detail in later chapters.

Divorce

Study of most civilizations shows that from the days of barbarism and primitive ways of life man and woman were able to live as "mixed", which involved mating without any constraints, satisfying lust while socializing. This aspect of human gathering gradually gave way to bonding and later evolved as a proper and legal form or marriage. The assumption was that marriage is a continuous and irrevocable contract. When it became obvious that in many cases the marriage contract cannot be permanent and hence its continuation may cause mental torture for either mates, a need arose for creating a legal framework to undo the arrangement. There were, therefore, provisions in law where divorce cases could more or less be foreseen.

Divorce in ancient Iran[6] was usually initiated as and when the husband decided so and it was not possible for the wife to intervene. Occasionally, however, the wife herself could have forced her husband to divorce. In the case that divorce was initiated by the husband and against the wishes of the wife, the husband would be obligated to return all generated income from her wealth or labor which he as head of family had stubbornly spent during their married life. Additionally, the wife could keep all or part of wealth that the husband had given to her at their wedding as well as gifts that he had endowed to her during their married life. If divorce had occurred with the consent of the wife she had no rights on either her past income or the wedding gifts. It is worth noting that in Iran as in Greece and Rome the father as the head of family had full authority to utilize all income he received from farm and real estate or wages earned, by women, men, slaves and all members of the family. The wealth of the family, in the first instance, would belong to the father and in the second instance, and with permission of the father, a small token of the wealth would be distributed among the wives and children.

Partnership of man and wife

During the *second historical* upheaval woman, in general, had no legal rights and could not be a party to any transactions either before or after marriage. Only after the husband was deceased and if there were no grown sons in the family, and only as a *Shah-zan* would she have the authority to conduct family affairs. During her married life she could only have independent legal rights if her husband, through a special legal procedures, had made her a partner in their financial affairs in which case the wife would have an independent legal status as a partner and could have an executive role, hence becoming a party to affirm and accept contracts and obligations.

In case of more than *one Shah-zan* in a family the husband could form separate partnerships with each one of them. Accordingly, each *Shah-zan* would share the profit and loss with her husband, but the income would be segregated for each wife. Such partnership could only be dissolved with the consent of the husband.

Veil

A thorough study of literary and arts belonging to various civilizations reveals that woman's veil has been a custom of ancient societies. Of course within the primitive and uncivilized tribes veil and even coverings had not existed, but among the more advanced people due to self promotion and love of luxurious articles the respected women would cover their faces. For sure, veil came to being, initially to protect the reverence of respectful women and later it became associated with chastity and modesty, mixed with religious ceremonies. The Greek women wore a veil as practiced in the isle of Coo[7].

A majority of Greek authors have written about use of veil by women. They include the daughter of Greek mythology King *Oileus* and women of city *Thebes*[8] who wore special veil with two small holes to accommodate their eyes to see. Spartan women, also practiced veils after marrying. The archeological discoveries in Greece and surroundings suggest that Spartan women covered their head, but left their faces exposed. Women and young girls often wore veils when shopping in public bazaar. In ancient Iran's religious environment respected women dressed modestly. To protect their upper class distinction and to create boundary and the limit with respect to "distinction" from the lower class they would cover their faces with long hair. In contrast ordinary women had short hair presumably for their physical and hard work which required agility that would make long hair unhelpful. Therefore the veil was exclusively reserved for women of the elite. Equally notable, this custom of covering had an appeal among the upper class women.

It should be noted that covering the face is absolutely not mandated by Islam religion. Since the advanced goal of this heavenly religion is to save the deprived and unfortunate women of the world it could not under any circumstances be in harmony with covering of woman's faces. Both the *Qur'an* and *Hadith* confirm the absence of any veil[9]. There is a fundamental difference between veil and denying women from demonstrating sensual suggestion which the *Qur'an* prescribes.

Wearing ornaments for the attention of public would make woman a desirable object. This contradicts the spirit of keeping women within the bounds of advanced teachings of Islam for their salvation and freedom from the chains of ignorance. Such high standard religious-inspired training would encompass and surpass all legal and social rights that man and woman can equally share.

CHAPTER SEVEN
Status of woman in Arabia before Islam

Murdering daughter- At the time that men of the relatively civilized nations of Rome, Greece, Iran and India refused to treat women as human beings, and denied them any financial transactions. At the same time they were actively exchanging them that included ownership and slavery. It should not, therefore, be surprising that in Arabia of Ignorance, a region at a stage of barbarism and savagery, fathers would bury alive their beautiful and delicate fruit of life, namely, their most innocent newborn daughters. This probably is registered as the most wrenching and vile event in the annals of treatment of woman in the world. Just to describe such horrendous story and its strangeness and cruelty would hurt readers' feelings. Just the thought of it will amaze the reader as to how an apparently normal person with a sound mind and without any anxiety or emergency and without feeling the slightest threat to his own life or caused by the child, would be capable of committing such unbelievable act of burying alive, with his own hands, a being that should normally radiate his life with joy as a part of himself.

How morally corrupt, how unfeeling, how debased and how wicked must a person be to commit murdering his newborn, that even a four legged wild animal would avoid, in absence of any imminent danger? To what extent could decadence and corruption influence man's mind so easily to commit such murderous crime without any cause? How could a community give its tacit approval by not expressing any emotional outrage?

The answer may be found after further tracking and study of the data that could reveal causes and, in turn, understanding of how the minds of these men worked at the time of committing such unthinkable act. Equally significant, the data could provide clues about the upbringing and living environment of these men. The widespread influencing factors throughout Arabia and similar regions of the world are summarized below.

1. Tightness of means of living and food shortages-

The living environment of an ignorant and primitive society, due to lack of know-how and required skill, for feeding a large group of people was unbearably difficult because such backward tribes were deprived from every source of wealth as well as the fundamental means of living, namely, handicrafts, farming and trade. Their handicraft ability was limited to knitting a rough rug-like material, in small quantities and fabricating some unattractive primitive living necessities. As for farming they could not be productive since they lacked the necessary tools and were ignorant of technical skills. As for trade, in addition to not having any products to trade, they were unfamiliar with basic principles as well as secrets of successful trading. The widespread poverty and impoverishment were the root cause of robbery and thievery which, in turn, created unsafe conditions on the roads as a necessary element of logistics.

Based on the above shortcomings, the responsibility of maintaining a large family, usually carried out by men, became such a heavy load that an ordinary man was unable to endure its subsequent hardship. On the other hand, ignorance and the primitive nature of tribes' traditions and culture did not allow the female members of a family to join the workforce. Such extra hand could have reduced the workload of the head of a family. For this reason and to reduce their pain of making a living, fathers contemplated avoidance of additional and unnecessary members of their family. Naturally, daughters became the easy prey because they had no protectors or representations except their own selfish and pitiless fathers filled with raw emotional anger. They became innocent victims of an environment of ignorance and foolishness; their fathers' supposed merciful feelings had gone awry. A mother's emotions ought, naturally and necessarily, to have protected her innocent children and have saved them from this tragic death.

Yet, in Tasmania[1] because of hardship and fear of going hungry and destitute she was resigned to accept the execution of her newborn daughters and to compensate and satisfy her feelings of motherhood with raising baby kittens and puppies.

In Australia[2] poverty and food scarcity among *aborigines,* on the one hand and bad education on the other hand, were the causes for an indiscriminate elimination of male or female children. The world traveller Stewart tells a horrific story about encountering an Australian man who smashed his three sick children heads with stone, then roasted their bodies on skewer and ate them[3]. In Sandwich island each family kept maximum of two or three children. The rest were either suffocated or buried alive.

In Tahiti island a religious group named *Aerois* would not allow its members to keep their children alive except the first born of the leaders of the group. Others including the ones who were respected or outstanding individuals were required to suffocate their children. In such tribes the girls who had survived were treated as the merchandise traded against worthless and useless items. The same people were reluctant to sell their sheep because they could make clothing from sheep wool, but what good would come of a girl? Killing a girl was a minor fault, far less important than hitting a female cow, producing milk.

In modern and socially advance island[4] of Taiwan until fifty years ago, women had no right to carry a child before reaching the age of thirty six. It was the civic and national duty of a believing woman to perform a forced abortion who had become pregnant before reaching the age of thirty six. Here of course the issue was not to prevent illegitimate birth or discourage lust and sensuality, but the government imposed strict rule intended to control the population due to insufficiency of food for the residents of the island.

2. Social structure and natural circumstances-

In Arabia of Ignorance (mostly illiterate nomads, ignorant of their surroundings) due to lack of central government there were many independent tribes, a collection of often lawless families. These people were mostly ignorant, hostile with various ethical deficiencies; the families were blood- enemies. A verse expresses this: "Two tribes were named *Kavoos* and *Khazra*'; one sought the other's blood "[5]. No security whether financial, personal or family protection existed; any tribe or family that was stronger or more opportunistic invaded the weaker group, mercilessly. Every male defendant had to shield his family members with one hand, and use his other hand to hold his sword for protecting them. In such chaotic environment it would obviously be easier to manage and protect smaller circle of members, reducing the chances of being caught off guard. The young men were naturally, and by training strong, well armed and capable of defending themselves, but protecting women who were delicate by nature and built with weaker body structure, due to both lack of nutrition and unhealthy growth, was a difficult and painful task for the father. This was another reason that motivated the father to bury the baby girl for relieving himself from the chores of feeding, nurturing and protecting her in such unfortunate life style.

The Eskimos of North America as well as Kamchatka (Eurasia) terminated child's life as soon as they discovered physical deficiencies in the newborn because struggling to live in that frozen and barren land was extremely difficult and those who were weak or with a disability could not easily survive. Two Eskimo women sold their children to Captain *Parry* for a few worthless pieces of belonging and immediately after transaction, stripped the children from their worn out clothing and seized their cloth, for they were more valuable than the children themselves. In Greenland they would bury a living child together with her dead mother. They believed that the mother would seek her child from *Khillo*, the place of dead people. It can be surmised that religion had justified the natural inclination of the community to reduce the number of consumers, as well as other local interests, to legitimize such inhuman behavior.

A South African tribe had experienced serious insecurity due to recent incidents of lions hurting human; they needed to be caught. To do so special traps were required to attract the lions usually a palatable meat. Some members of a neighboring tribe accommodated this by killing young children and providing the necessary bait[6] for them.

3. Bad education, selfishness and foolishness:

The spiteful and ignorant communities who lack resources while having a low level of civility, knowledge and education, even by ignoring the first two aforementioned deficiencies (items1 and 2), and purely due to illusion *(vahm)* and superstition their response to the slightest provocation of anger and lust is to commit murder. There is no self-virtue, honor and dignity that would lead their emotions and feeling towards goodness. Even the least animalistic feelings that may exist between creatures and their children have become more intense and harsh in these tribes so much that they consider paying attention and nurturing of their children, who are part of themselves, a burden to themselves and the enemy of their comfort and indulgence. They destroy these heavenly gifts so easily and with no feelings of remorse or hesitation in their minds at all. The cause of burying the child with his or her dead mother is that they are not willing to forego their seeking pleasure through sensual desire. They do not want to disrupt their so-called peace of mind and their relaxation in lieu of caring for their orphan child and other members of the family.

How much can a man, this heavenly being, this miracle and this generous gift who is the symbol of the production from the beginning of the book of creation, become so low and wicked and degenerate? How can a man as father be so void of feelings to bury alive an innocent, faultless and hopeless creature, born as a part of him and having no one except her father to protect her from everyday difficulties and calamities? How misfortunate and sinister it is when, frightened by and fearful of demonic death, a child who always responds to her father with a sweet smile and affection, a smile that tells the story of secrets of love with heavenly kindness and true sincerity, is confronted with brute force.

Byron, while traveling observed a primitive Native American-Indian from the tribe *Fuegie* setting up a bonfire, throwing his child on steel skewer making himself a barbecue. His only crime was that he had dropped and wasted a basket of eggs[7].

The wild tribes, from India and Sri Lanka to the Himalayas also murdered their daughters. Even Indian aristocrats, the Rajas, committed such crimes. In their view having an unmarried daughter was a disgrace and marrying her to people of lower class was equally disdainful. The ideal husband from upper class would demand an expensive dowry and worse, they did not take a good care of their wives; therefore it was preferable not to have any daughters.

How could poverty, or chaotic social situations, or bad education be sufficient for a man, with normal and natural state of mind, murder his child? No matter how low and corrupt a man behaves due to bad education and training; no matter how weak his tribe's feelings are and in the absence of any virtue and goodness, could it still be possible for a man to become so debased and dispassionate, beneath the level of a wild animal, to commit such atrocities?

Could it still be possible that a murder is committed by a human, when a four-legged animal refuses to commit, even when he is in danger of elimination and realizes that his salvation is contingent upon giving up his child? Even if the animal's life could be saved by fleeing, the creature would be unwilling to do so and leave his child unprotected; he would prefer to die with his child. Yet, a man with no sense of danger and without any necessity or compelling reason does not hesitate to commit such a crime.

Animals feelings

In a recent fire that took place in France, a female corvine bird unable to fly out her children to safety did not attempt to fly alone, but stayed until she was enveloped in the flames of fire with her children. During the 1871 war between France and Prussia, a cannon bullet exploded inside a storage area, but it did not cause a female pigeon who was laying egg to make any move[8]. Mammals demonstrate their feelings and emotions even more intensely. In Central Africa a female elephant, surrounded and about to be caught by *Livingston* hunting party[9], was energetically expressing her affection to her child by touching her with her trunk hiding her under her belly. In Sumatra, Indonesia, an Orangutan female monkey chased by captain Hall was running with her child. She was observed to be attempting to place her child on the highest tree branch available, as she was bleeding from a bullet wound; watching and warning her child of any danger and continually encouraging the child to flee until her last breadth[10]. Stories and related narratives to prove the phenomenon of animals feelings abound, the above-mentioned anecdotes should suffice to make the point. The only explanation that can be assumed to be a reason for an ignorant human race to descend to such low level of existence as compared to animals can be surmised as follows.

Initially, the tenderness and the nature of feelings as related to degraded human races and tribes were little different from that of the four-legged animals. It is also known there is no positive correlation between feelings and intelligence- actually in most cases there is a negative one. The power of intelligence and thinking are, however, prerequisite for prediction which ensures future well being. This matter of expectation is intensified much more in humans, than in animals regardless of moral standing. Therefore man, contrary to animal, can make a series of predictions. An increase of family size results in more people to feed and educate followed by more unpalatable consequences. Next it is the matter of marrying the daughters which will cause more suffering of mind and the physical pain. By marrying off daughters to outside of the family, their (family) integrity and social standing will suffer as viewed by public opinion. All in all, the livelihood, comfort and peace of mind of man will suffer.

Furthermore, man is not committed to the fundamentals and principles of education and training to ease or offset the burden that he would endure in educating his children; he lacks honor and virtue that would prevent him from committing a crime. That is why even under an appropriate circumstance and in absence of any impediments one may not expect anything from him other than committing criminal acts. It is worth noting that among the animals who are more intelligent than others, with some similarities to spiteful and base humans, child killing has been observed. Chimpanzee of *Ouistiti* is of a type who gets tired of taking along his child and decide to "eat" his head, by striking him hard against a tree and throwing away the child's headless body[11].

In any case, the women and young girls in Arabia of Ignorance suffered the most. As viewed by fathers and husbands, the young daughters and wives were weak creatures, worthless and something that could be owned and traded as merchandise. Their treatment of young girls manifests the sorry state of woman's social status and prestige. If mothers had any authority or influence their feelings and motherly affection would have never allowed the father to bury her innocent young daughters alive. This natural right of women, universally observed within families of any civilized society, has been the missing link. Killing of young daughters in Arabia shows that the father had unlimited power while the mother was not even permitted to have any sayings in the conduct of daily family affair.

Of course this crime of daughter killing was not extended to all families in Arabia. Some families, influenced by morally inspired teachings stayed away from this wicked practice. Similarly, factors such as wealth, certain inherited cultural traditions and nobility prevented some tribes, such as *Ghoreeish*, from committing this inhuman and shameful crime.

History of daughter killing

Apparently, the first tribe that committed this crime was *Bani-Tamim* Tribe. *Ne'man-Ibn-Monzar* the king of *Hyereh* who was provoked by this tribe on one occasion, dispatched his brother *Dyan-Ibn-Monzar* to suppress the tribe. By doing so, he took many prisoners, mostly women and young girls of the tribe. Sometime later the leaders of *Bani-Tamim* Tribe came to *Ne'man*, apologizing for their past actions and begged for mercy and forgiveness. At last, *Ne'man* pitied them and ordered every prisoner who wished to rejoin her husband or her father to be freed and anyone wished to stay could do so. Some of the women chose to stay, notably the daughter of *Gheis-Ibn-Aasem*. Her captor, *Omar-Ibn-Alshamrokh-al-shokry* volunteered to marry her and live with her. *Gheis* was angered by this humiliation and vowed that from then on he will bury his new born daughters[12]. Others followed him in earnest.

Sa'sa'-et-Ibn-Najieh Tamimi was in search of his two lost baby camels. He came to a house where he inquired from the owner about his lost camels. The answer was affirmative, but right at that time the wife was delivering a baby that turned out to be a girl. The angry father decided to suffocate the newborn girl. *Sa'sa'* offered to buy the new born girl, but the father refused because selling a child, he believed, was a disgrace.

At last *Sa'sa'* and the father agreed that in exchange for saving the life of the new born girl, *Sa'sa' would* turn over the two baby camels plus the one he was riding on[13].

Some Arab tribes beheaded the new born girls, some would throw down the baby from a hilltop and some would just drown the baby. Generally, the root of the killing of new born girls was the fear of poverty and lack of means of sustenance. Prophet of Islam at the onset of his Coming warned Arabs against this tragic crime and assured them that God will provide sustenance or daily bread for their daughters:

"Whoever gives tooth, also provides bread[14]".

Furthermore, the belief in a mix of fear and superstition has a share in creating this situation. Educating and nurturing a young girl and submitting her to a male outside the family as husband in Arabs view are incompatible with honor, dignity and bravery of a man and his family. Birth of a daughter was considered a bad omen and having a daughter was inauspicious. Accordingly, the news about the birth of a daughter would infuriate a man. Those uncivilized tribes who did not value their women the same as men considered the addition of another daughter to be a heavy burden on their family and tribe; hence unwelcome.

Truly, the Prophet of Islam conferred a great favor to humanity and in particular woman and more specifically to Arabian women. Not only did he save them from a wretched death, but he gave them the rights to enjoy a social livelihood and standing by gaining equal rights in many aspects of their lives. A woman who was traded or exchanged for a four-legged animal was now given the rights to own and trade by herself. Today, the position of woman makes no distinction between son and daughter and having a daughter in a family is no longer unfortunate. Such privileges were quite advanced when presented and practiced fourteen hundred years ago by the Prophet of Islam. The learned people and leadership of Islam when informed of the good news that a child was born did not inquire of the sex of the child; instead they would ask if the child was healthy and defect-free. If the baby was in full health, they would prostrate and thank God repeatedly.

Consequence of killing girls

The result of killing new born girls in Arabia of Ignorance was the gradual reduction of female population; so much that three to four men had to share one woman at a time. This ugly and shameful type of marriage was known as *Zamad.* A woman after giving birth would gather all her husbands and depending on facial similarity she would identify the biological father of the child. One can well imagine what the level of integrity and the worth of such woman would be. Under what ethical and moral standards would this child be raised? How worthy was the nurturing and feeding of the child by such a woman?

Teachings of Islam effectively increased the number of women to the extent that female to male ratio reversed itself creating the condition that polygamy was allowed, but only under certain conditions as detailed in Part II.

Regarding divorce in Arabia, the woman's unfortunate condition was no better than marriage. A man who had divorced his wife solely at his own volition without cause, reason or rationale had the right to re-possess her at will and repeatedly. There was no limit to this vicious circle of divorce and remarrying the same woman. The wife was treated like a ball in the hand of the game player. Islam limited this act of remarrying to two times.

The next chapter will explore the important contribution that Islam's advanced teaching, has made on nurturing and educating women by raising their moral and mental standard. This manifested itself in an amazing transformation of nurturing of the mothers and brave women in all social aspects and walks of life throughout the Muslim world.

CHAPTER EIGHT
Status of woman after Islam

Influence of parents in a family

The understanding of how the teachings of Islam leads to the transformation of society's social fabric along with the improvement of the living standards of its people, in the first place, hinges on Islam making an all-out effort to advance the position of woman. To comprehend this, one notes that the criterion and reference to the prestige and the strength of a community is dependent on the particulars of morals and the level of general education of the members of that community, which is a cluster of families formed by its members. These communities form towns and collectively a nation. In other words, the foundation of civil society of every country is based on the strength and the health of its foundation or the structure of families at national level.

The executive members including the managing director in every family are the parents of the children. Father is responsible for the subsistence as well as all financial undertakings for the family and generally meet the needs of the family. Mother is in charge of educating and nurturing the children who are earmarked for future leadership of the country. Mother's share in education and training includes, building of a foundation for teaching the children moral principles necessary for their proper nurturing. This responsibility is considerably more significant and harder than that of the father. It is her embraces and her extended arms that form the primary schooling for the child to learn the meaning of love. This plays a key role in the quality of child's morals. The moral and mental quality of mother is passed onto the child blood through mother's blood and milk.

Mutual relations of matter and spirit

Nurturing the child in mother's womb and later in her arms and feeding the child through her blood followed by her milk is an important topic that must be carefully studied because undoubtedly, material and spiritual tendencies work in opposite direction. This concept is exemplified below.

In a city in central part of Iran, most of the buildings are made of dried mud which is extracted from its hard and sticky soil. Although the city's many structures have been constructed hundred of years ago, they are still sound and will probably last a long time. This hardness and adhesiveness are passed onto residents of the city through grains and other produce of the city, directly affecting city residents' mental conditions and needs. As the saying goes, their upbringing makes them ungenerous and parsimonious to the extent that *Saheb-Ibn- Ebad* prior to entering that town told his people, "ask me now whatever you wish; otherwise upon entering this town I will be excused to honor your request". The meaning is that he will be subjected to the same conditioning as the residents and hence niggardly. There is, therefore, no doubt about the transfer of material property, in the form of chemistry, onto human spirit and vice versa.

After this introduction, the importance of the influence of mother's morals as well as mother's education in nurturing the child becomes evident and the relationship of a man with his mother should not be overlooked. It is rare to impossible that great men have followed other than great women. Before the introduction of Islam, the tribes that were uncivilized and the idolators were completely unaware of the effects of education and nurturing. The civilized nations, too, did not pay much attention to anything other than just educating men while, generally, woman was of no value except for reproduction and satisfying man's lust.

Islam directed the attention of civilized nations to the fact that reproducing a generation, one after another, is a common denominator between human and animal. What distinguishes human is his proper education; otherwise a woman and a viviparous cat are not different. A verse of Islamic teaching says:

"Discipline of a family is based on the discipline of the mother; a woman is the foundation and principle discipline of her family:

Therefore woman's advanced (as opposed to lagged behind) intellectual thinking would influence the advancement of a society. Conversely, her lagged intellect would contribute to society's backwardness. Woman is a mirror to the family, that is, ethical motivation or wickedness in woman would translate to morality or immorality in the family. It is impossible for a society to contain good people and or bad people without a sample (of good or bad) within a family. As a consequence, the progress and ascent of women in a society will be instrumental in advancement of that society, and conversely degeneration and immorality of women would lead to the beginning of decline of that society.

There is a causal agent in a woman that flourishes if she is educated correctly and it is combined with freedom as prescribed by good sense. Woman is an influencing agent, not only within the family circle, but also in cooperation with man striving in all aspects of social life; otherwise, it must be said that her endowed intellect, faculties and understanding (similar to man) have been in vain and hence worthless. In

61

particular, woman is stronger and more active in charity affairs and public welfare because her natural instinct, tender sentiments and heart felt emotion would enable her to physically withstand the difficulty of caring for a sick and injured and orphans willingly, but a woman who is not educated and has not had a leader would waste her qualities in worthless matters and extravagance.

Woman's attribute

Women of early Islam were involved in community welfare. Narratives in social matters, news and religious and discourse have been recorded by number of the Prophet's wives, the great women of their time as female companions of Prophet. Many Moslem women excelled in science and literature. *Am Attieh* is quoted to have said: "I participated in battles of *Seven-Ghazaveh* alongside the Prophet and in all seven battles I prepared food for soldiers of Islam. I baked bread, and I medicated and nursed the injured soldiers." There is no difference between this Moslem woman and today's western women who dedicated their lives to serving mankind.

Contributions of Islam to woman's cause

Islam transformed woman's position in Arabia of Ignorance, initially by prohibiting the murder of new born daughters, and then began the process of building respect for woman. The reason behind the Prophet's repeated kissing his daughter's hand (as a sign of full respect) was to make daughters and wives, in view of their fathers and husbands, respectable individuals. Later, Islam prohibited adultery encouraging and promoting, instead, marriage. It is interesting to note that in defining marriage, Islam has stressed the importance of woman and has established the social equality of woman with man[1]. Islam, in effect, applied the art of persuasion for respecting woman.

Islam has founded the elegant structure of marriage on the basis of love and mercy, but unfortunately in many Muslim countries it has gradually been reduced to mostly a ceremonial affair through which man is allowed to use a woman merely for his physical pleasure[2]. Such application is quite different from what Islam religion teaches.

The definition of marriage as stated in the Qur'an, contains thousands of literary and philosophical secrets. "Love and mercy" in marriage and equality of two parties of the contract attest to a committed devotion and sincerity between the two parties. The prelude to love is an intense attraction to each other which means that the two persons must meet each other before marriage in order to understand each others feelings and moral values. That is why Islam is the only religion recommending that man should look directly at the bride-to-be before any ceremony. The Prophet is quoted to have said to one of his aids before his marriage ceremony:

"Look at your woman; and may God maintain warm feelings between the two of you."

- Islam has given equal rights to man and woman in their marriage[3]. *Omar-Ibn- al-Khattab*[4] is quoted as saying (to men): "After faith nothing is better for a believing servant of God than pious woman"

- Another improvement made to marriage affair was to prohibit re -marrying of the wife of the father, either after the husband was deceased as a sign of respect for fathers.

- Marrying two sisters is prohibited to prevent grudging or indignation.

- On the subject of divorce, as mentioned before, the right of man to revoke the divorce was limited both in terms of the period allowed and the number of times that could be repeated.

On another front, Islam prohibited the blameworthy practices which contradicted generosity: "do not pressure the woman to give up part or all of her material possessions(*Sedagh)* "[5].

Islam has valued worshipping of the woman the same as that of a man; whereas some religions including Judaism, Buddhism and Brahman make a distinction in this regard. In Judaism, woman is not accepted as witness and her oath is not accepted. She also cannot make a vow and, as in ancient Iranian beliefs, woman was forced to be isolated in a segregated building during her monthly period. She was not allowed to speak to anyone and was forced to eat by herself. Her dress was considered unclean and the servants who were taking her food and drinks had to cover their mouth and nose with thick cloths as protection against the unclean air in the designated confined area.

Islam delivered woman from all such deplorable situations[6] placing man and woman at the same standing. Islam reminds men (and women) of treating their parents with beneficence.

Prophet has said to fathers: "When you purchase something (gifts for children) you have to offer the present first to girl(s) because their feelings are more sensitive to hurt". Additionally, "Woman is honorific and no one except the mean one is insolent towards her".

Inheritance:
Even though all previous religions had denied inheritance to women, Islam provided, in the 7th century, the legal rights for women to share family's inheritance, from husband, children, brother, sister, father and all relatives of the family[7].

Influence of woman in nurturing the child
The major significance of motherhood that Islam attributes to woman is her upbringing of children. As discussed before, the topic of nurturing a child begins from mother's womb, feeding the child through blood and milk and continually holding the child close to the body (i.e., mother's arms, chest and lap). These are very important phases of nurturing that must not be neglected.

Ghazali, an Iranian philosopher and thinker of 12th century aptly describes nurturing of a child:

"...child is entrusted from God and is endowed unto parents. The child's pure heart is a precious gem, plain and untouched by any design of (paintings) impression, worthy of being drawn on its surface and leaning towards what the child may want to gravitate. If he is guided to goodness and well being he will be happy and will prosper in this world and the next to come. As such, the parents, trainers and teachers will share his success. If he is pushed to mischief and corruption and his education and training has been neglected or ignored he will be unfortunate and wretched. The sinful subsequent of death of soul and body will be borne by the child's guardian and master. God has made parents and teachers responsible for safeguarding of the family members and children, from hell".

A child's plain soul at his early age is exposed and vulnerable to ugly as well as beautiful painting vision. His education, however, takes shape among women of the family and relatives starting with the child's mother. It can be concluded, therefore, that the child's upbringing is directly influenced by morality of family members.

Occurrence and antiquity

According to some of the late philosophers an individual's soul is created simultaneously with his body; that is, the soul is time-dependent. After death the soul survives. Previously it was thought that the relative, or an individual soul, was time-dependent as was an absolute soul. This meant that the soul's status, prior to belonging to a body, of felicity or misery (and curse) would be assured and it is unchangeable. Not so. The late philosophers believe that only absolute soul is ancient and unchangeable, but the individual or relative soul is attached to body and is created at the same time as the body. Accordingly, the soul of an individual begins with sperm formation and creation of fetus. Here is an interpretation of a known Arabic proverb:

"If a person is created from a healthy and pure fetus within the uterus of chaste and pious woman and is fed from mother's noble milk and later continue to be fed by mother's milk, or from the milk of a chaste woman nurse, his soul will be pure and pious; otherwise a wretched and vicious person".

Just as the child's level of (blood) purity at birth depends on that of the mother's quality of fetus and uterus, as well as the overall parents' health and temperament, his happiness and well being will also depend on parents spiritual impression of the child's newly embedded soul in fetus within the womb. It is this observation that concludes that human inherits temperaments. Noting that materialism and spiritualism are in opposite poles, pure blood and milk affect the quality of the created child's spiritual and mental condition. For this reason Islam religion values greatly the goodness of mother as the most important factor in delivering a well nurtured child.

On the topic of marriage, Islam mandates that by paying the utmost attention to the health of body and soul of the wife and her family one should firstly look for her moral values and honor and secondly, observe that woman has no physical defect or an incurable disease. Further, man should not treat the mother-to-be with insolence during her pregnancy and in the entire period of child suckling nor should he demean the nurse. (In choosing the nurse, she must have a good appearance with perfect health.)

In short, a pious woman with family of good morals, healthy and with no physical defects will produce a pure fetus from the loin of father with good will and right mind, placed in mother's cleansed womb, that being fed with pure blood and milk of mother ultimately deliver a pious, brave and mature individual to the society. The above sections summarize the nurturing process of a child based on teachings of Islam.

Nourishment

It is worth mentioning that Islam stressed so much on nurturing of the child that every factor that could influence the child's upbringing is explained in detail. No other religions or laws prior to Islam addressed the subject of nourishing of a child. Islam, for the first time, mapped out a special topic of child nourishment, followed by prescribed rules based on specified law. Islam considered the effects of nourishment being comparable to those of parental lineage.

Adoption of son

It is appropriate to note another improvement that Islam has made in the family affairs. In Arabia of Ignorance as in the most civilized societies, adopting son(s) was a routine matter for the purpose of maintaining the family lineage. As noted before, in ancient Rome, Greece and Iran the families who had no sons would accept another family's son as their own son where all the rules for a natural son would be equally applied to the adopted son. That meant he would inherit the same as the biological son and all the confidents of his adopted father would be his confidents too. Marrying the divorced wife of the adopted son was not permitted just as the case of biological son's. The basic reason was that a real family relationship was assumed only to exist between fathers and sons. Women were so inferior and worthless that men were not prepared to accept family lineage between father and daughter or mother and son. Surviving daughters for the sake of name and continuity of her father and father's family were not sufficient at all.

Islam disagreed with these procedures for two reasons. First there was a lack of respect for women; second, the habit was against the laws of nature and therefore unacceptable. That is why the Prophet named the two sons of his daughter his own sons.

The principle of blood relation and blood-sameness is respected in Islam. As shall be seen later on the subject of Inheritance, the basis of dividing inheritance in Islam is similar to Roman and Greek, but contrary to Germanic laws; it maintain blood and blood-sameness relationship. Accordingly, it will be against the laws of nature if the inheritance of the deceased is given to a person who does not carry the same blood and merely is an adopted son. That is the reason the deceased cannot draw a will giving more than one third of his inheritance to other than legal survivors. A will that endows more than one-third of the inheritance to one individual must have the signed approval and the consent of all inheritors; otherwise the will is considered void.

While not contesting the tradition of adoption, Islam made a distinction between adopted and actual sons. This simple, yet important, matter had no cause or motive except as a practical abolition of a wrong habit practiced by Arabs which had taken a strange twist. The case is detailed below.

Zeinab was the niece of the Prophet, an orphan nurtured by the Prophet from childhood. As a preamble, there was no veil, for covering face at that time for Prophet not to view her features and secondly if there was any veil, certainly no directive was issued prior to *Zeinab* reaching puberty. The Prophet had nurtured her under his own care and therefore he had fully seen and known her. If he wanted to marry her there was nothing to prevent him and it would have been preferable and more desirable as an untouched and chaste woman than a widow. Prestige and greatness of Prophet at the time was so much that any woman of nobility and respectability would be honored to be his wife. *Khadije*, the wealthiest and most established woman in Arabia had married him prior to his call for being the Messenger of God. Marrying *Zeinab* needed no introduction and no preparation.

The Prophet desired to abolish the centuries old wrong habits embedded in Arabs' souls; they did not believe that adopted son was different from real son. To show them otherwise, the Prophet decided to wed *Zeinab*, who was under his care and supervision, with *Zeid* whom he had "adopted" as his own son. This marriage was not that easy because *Zeinab* and her brother were of *Qureish* family, considered of nobility in Arabia; whereas *Zeid* was son of a slave hence without family prestige. *Zeid*, aware of his status, knew that living with a woman who was socially superior to him and of a family of honor, virtue and lineage would be difficult, hence unwilling to marry *Zeinab*. The Prophet ordered both to obey his wish and from his personal funds, paid the required amount to the bride at the wedding ceremony on behalf of the bridegroom. The marriage took place, but as expected it did not last long. *Zeinab's* constant sense of superiority led to *Zeid's* expressing his unhappiness to Prophet who, in turn, would give him advice to be patient. At last he succeeded in obtaining Prophet's consent to divorce *Zeinab*. After divorce, the Prophet married *Zeinab* to demonstrate the wrong habit of Arabs. In this manner the Prophet made the Arabs understand that how adopted son would differ from the biological son. Father of an adopted son *can* marry the divorced wife of his adopted son, but not the divorced wife of his biological son.

The Prophet had already laid out a plan for implementing his intention. He had foreseen that marriage of *Zeinab* and *Zeid* would not last long. Specifically he chose a wife for *Zeid* who first of all, would be under his supervision and obey his instructions; second, in view of circumstances which have been mentioned, the parties would not be so attracted to each other that breakup of marriage ties would not be a cause for their concern nor contrary to morality and fairness. Of course the aim had been this important mission; otherwise the Prophet's marrying any woman unmarried or divorced would have been a great honor to her family. There would have been no point for the Prophet to have married *Zeinab* who was, before her marriage to *Zeid*, under his care and supervision to have suddenly after her marriage become interested in her and have *Zeid*, out of respect for Prophet's wishes, divorce her so that the Prophet could marry her.

Islam, the religion of truth, with its advanced social thoughts, revolutionized the world by delivering woman from the misery of being despised. Islam laid the family foundation on affection, kindness, justice and fairness. For nurturing children, Islam teaches and trains an educated and pious mother. Freedom and respect that were endowed to women by

Islam would greatly enhance the grounding of mothers' qualification and her ability to nurture a child.

Man and woman are considered "adults" both materially and physically, if they are able to re-generate. Similarly, with regards to moral and intellectual training both father and mother are considered adults who are capable of nurturing brave and competent children. Mothers who were trained under the banner of Islam were able to nurture children who dominated most of the world of their period, exporting their national and religious customs and traditions throughout the world. They considered death as the least danger on the road to success and fearing death, the biggest shame.

Based on the above, more efforts than ever must be made towards educating and training of women, young and old, with no stone unturned, in order for a society to deliver outstanding, brave, honest and committed who demonstrate their ability to immune and safeguard fellow citizens' dignity as well as society's political, social structure from any danger.

CHAPTER NINE
Status of women among
uncivilized tribes

The effects of civilization and culture as well as the contributions made to humanity by religious leaders, reformers and thinkers may be understood by appreciating the extent of the guidance that religious leaders, especially the Prophet of Islam have envisaged and applied to societies, particularly to women.

Not long ago and before today's social status of women in modern societies, one must recall that the topics described in previous chapters regarding woman's situation in ancient civilizations of Rome, Greece and others were not fantasies, since even now (late 19th century) some savage tribes and idolators live in extreme destitute and despicable situations at the level of four legged pets and load-carrying animals; these people are ignorant of civilization as well as heavenly religions. Although in the past two centuries these tribes have been subdued and their lands have been occupied by major world powers and as a result the living conditions of women along with their social welfare have somewhat improved. There is reduced barbarism and violence, but most of the superstitious habits still persist, some with the intensity of ancient days as detailed in following sections.

Dominating the weak through strength

Basically, in human gatherings the thoughts of recognizing right from wrong, spreading justice, feelings of mercy and kindness towards the weak and the oppressed are characteristics of superior teachings and advanced civil societies. These thoughts and feelings are totally foreign and unreal in violent and barbaric tribes whose members resemble hellish demons. As a result, since all over the world women are always weaker than men one must expect that her destiny is determined by the law of "domination of strong over the weak". The more violent and primitive the tribe or group, the harsher and more definitive the influence and power of above-mentioned law. Accordingly, it can be stated that the position and status of women in every society in terms of grace and violence, represent the level of civility and mentally undeveloped society.

Women in Australia

In Australia woman is treated as a pet whose only use is for satisfying man's lust and reproducing the next generation. In the past she had another application which is now abolished because of their proximity to civilization in certain areas. In those days, when frequent draughts resulted in famine they would kill the women and eat her flesh. The main profession of man was fighting and hunting. As nomads in the deserts the wife and the children had to carry their bare belongings while accompanying the husband. Women would busy themselves by fishing on the river banks, providing the basic component of nutrition for the family, but women was not allowed to dine with the men in the family. She would have to wait until her husband and other men were finished eating and if anything was left she could feed herself and other females of the family. Marriage of these tribes was nothing but continuing act of fornication. The husband or master of woman did not show slightest kindness or affection towards the woman in his heart. Woman was an object and a very inexpensive one at that. A famous church minister, Rev. Pere Salvado, in his book[1] tells a story that one early evening a very laud uproar and an intense fight was heard. "The women cries were terrifying. I ran after the noise. Eight women had gathered around the fireplace in the kitchen, fighting intensely with heavy clubs. My advices and attempt to mediate among these savage animals was not helpful; at last using my steel cane, I struck a few times on the shoulders and shoulder blades of two of the most wicked ones to be able to separate them and end the fighting that had resulted in several broken skulls and injured shoulder blades, while blood was running everywhere." The interesting part of story is that the husbands were sitting by the side of the kitchen with the least amount of caring and quite calm, laughing at this bloody quarrel. "With total amazement I asked them how was it that they were sitting there watching their wives nearly murdering each other. They responded: Do you expect us to interfere in some women in-fighting? I said what if one of them is actually killed what would you do? With a ridiculous laugh they said: There is nothing to it. If one dies there are a thousand more women for us."

Usually, upon the death of husband, and after three days are passed the woman will belong to husband's brother. It is interesting to note that Australian woman rarely dies of natural cause. In general prior to coming of the fixed term of her death, when she becomes ill with total disregard and care her dying accelerates, and sometime with no prior illness the man suffocates her. That is because if she is allowed to live, as she gets older, she will eat a considerable amount of "others" food stuff.

Women of Fiji Island

A French philosopher's[2] observations[3] of the habits and customs of people of Fiji Island is worth mentioning here. The people of this island, based on their affectionate feelings towards their parents, bury them when they reach the age of forty in order to spare them old age, when they become weak and decrepit. At a designated time and place of burial all the family members will quite happily gather and the wretched victims, who want to travel to the world of spirits, after bidding farewell to each family member and friends, lie still in the grave dug for them and the sons cover the top of the grave after filling it with dirt. This custom is not meant to represent cruelty and ruthlessness, but it is interpreted as an act of goodness. The reason for selecting age of forty, is that they believe it is approximately the middle of natural age and the most matured age of man's life and that the deceased will be raised from the grave on the Day of Resurrection with the same physical condition of strength and maturity."

In the same island man can sell his wife or kill her. Often, the unfortunate women, for the most minor fault, are tied to the trunk of a tree and whipped. In New Caledonian woman does not have the right to eat in presence of a man; even her dwelling is separated. Yet, the heaviest daily chores in life are her share of responsibility.

As mentioned before, since the underlying of different uncivilized tribes' behavior is the similar to each other, their habits and rituals are also identical. Specifically, in treating women clearly no noticeable differences can be found. The criteria and the source is the familiar weakness and helplessness that have embroiled women with oppression at the hands of men. The situation of an African woman is not at all better than that of South Pacific islands. It just happens that most part of Africa is fertile land and hunting ground and most African men are shepherds or farmers and as a result there is plenty of food. As a result men are less tempted to eat woman than in the South Pacific. Nevertheless, the British explorer, Sir Samuel Baker[4] in his documentary tells the story about a festivity held on the banks of Upper Nile and the prepared food for the guests contained meat extracted from innocent black African women and children.

African women

In most parts of Africa, erecting a structure, weaving a mat-like rug and or carpet, plowing, planting and irrigation are all woman's jobs and men are not willing to make any contribution or assist at all. In some places even more skilled professions such as hairdressing, medical related operations and transporting goods are performed by women. Men usually choose only tailoring, dry cleaning and sometime, metalworking for themselves. Generally, jobs reserved for men are considered noble and respectable; for example in South Africa, blacksmith is considered a respectable profession and he is called "doctor of iron"; blacksmith profession is assumed to bear technical and industrial skill, and at times, creates political weight for such men. In Central Africa like South Pacific Islands, woman is not permitted to eat with her husband. The children pay absolutely no attention to their mother and the father of the family strikes his wife to the point of death with the slightest excuse. The amazing thing is that the unlucky wife considers this situation fair and she does not complain at all.

In the more civilized areas of Africa the daily chores of women are not less than other black African tribes. In Senegal as well as Darfur, now part of Sudan, wife must hold her husband's stirrup for mounting[5]. Many black women of this land are seen carrying food stuffs and heavy bushels of wheat, walking along their husband and master who usually rides a donkey. As a token of appreciation the husbands sell them for pocket change or a "gift" to strangers.

Polynesian women
There is a significant difference in terms of freedom and sensuality between a single woman and married woman in Polynesian islands. Young women before marriage can go anywhere in any manner and have relationships with anybody, committing every kind of obscene act. As soon as they marry they will become just like a "farm property" that would be under the firm control of the of "property owner". No one is now allowed to touch or violate her newly established rights without the consent of her owner. For this reason the wife is forced, in accordance with her husband's wishes, to sleep with anyone he sees fit. In most islands, the woman is required to prepare the food for her husband, or

collect fruit from the forest, often under extreme hardship, or go fishing on the river banks, waist deep in the water with burning sun, shining on her unprotected face, standing for hours. Here again, like the previous cases, woman has to wait until her husband has finished eating before she and her daughters can eat if anything is left to eat. Additionally, man's clothes, weapons and hat are considered so sacred for the wife and daughters that they are not allowed to touch them; specially men's head is sanctified in a particular manner and women are not allowed to pass through from the side of their heads when they are asleep.

In Marquesas Islands[6] delicious foods such as chickens, pigs, coconut and walnut are named heavenly foods. These foods are reserved for gods and men and women have neither rights nor avidity to it. Permission to eat ham in Christianity was the most important factor for the women of these islands to embrace that religion. In *Rapanui* Island women had to hand feed their men. In New Zealand weight carrying is reserved for women and it is considered a denigration of man's dignity and prestige.

Women in North Pole, America[7]

Within the uncivilized tribes in frozen North Pole, in all seasons of the year and even in the middle of brutal winter the helpless women are forced to go in the water whether for fishing or emptying water out of the already immersed fishing boats. Building special glacial hut and boat rowing are the specialized jobs of women. Even women while pregnant or nursing a newborn are not exempt from these hardships. Nursing mothers must carry her newborn child wrapped in a hind, on her back while working. Men work a few hours of hunting in a week and spend the rest of the week on recreation and amusement. For such services and forced labor, during periods of famine they suffocate the older women who no longer can work effectively, and eat their flesh.

Suffocating of women

The method of suffocating consists of placing woman's head in a pit filled with smoked charcoal and firewood. Her head is held forcefully until she is dead[8]. Most tribes mentioned here protect themselves from the danger of enemy from routine theft and surprise attack by setting up night watch. The execution of this important task also rests with women who have been subjected to the hardship and difficulties of their daily chores. Men sleep peacefully at night while women must set up a fire and maintain a watch until dawn.

Strange custom

In one of the savage tribes on the Caribbean Islands there is a habit that cannot be explained even as childish. In most human societies when a woman gives birth she should rest a while; the period and quality of which varies depending on the level of civilization, environmental condition, natural necessities and physical conditions of the woman. In the tent-dweller and nomadic tribes, due to lack of means of resting and woman's constitutional strength as well as her inferior status and social irrelevancy, it is possible to deny her the right to rest and as has been observed, force her to immediately resume her work. However, in this tribe a strange and amazing custom is practiced. Immediately upon the birth of the child and woman's resumption of work the husband begins a convalescence period, resting comfortably in bed while being attended by physician and medicated[9] accordingly.

Asian women

In the relatively civilized Asian societies, the status of women is no better. For example, in Tibet and China even though women are not considered the carrier of physical goods throughout their lives they remain under the guardianship of their father or husband as far as social rights are concerned. Until several years ago (and still in some parts of China)[10] marriage was a simple trade manifestation. In China woman does not have the right to eat with her husband or sons. Woman at the dining table is just furniture. She sits motionless and silent, only to light up her husband's pipe. Her food will be the leftover of male members of family. Daughters usually do not share inheritance; instead a modest dowry is provided for them as part of the marriage ceremony.

Women in Indochina

In Indochina and Burma woman testimony is ineffective. Women must not contaminate the place of the court with their unclean presence(as in ancient Rome). In special cases that woman's testimony is accepted and effective they must stand at the entrance door to give their testimony. The Burmese men have the right to loan their wives to strangers. In the event that husband or father becomes the debtor, complaint is filed against the wife and it is possible that creditor accept favors from her in lieu of money.

Women in India

In India, a Hindi woman is under the control of her father before her marriage. During her married life, she obeys her husband and if divorced or widowed she will obey her son. If she has no sons she will obey her father's relations and in the absence of that she will be obedient to the current king. These persons mentioned are considered by her as god. The husband addresses his wife as servant and female-slave. Conversely, she must address her as mister, master, your excellency and sometime *lord*. At any event it is prohibited for wife to mention husband's name. Woman is not allowed to be educated. For Hindi women during their monthly period, as mentioned in previous chapters, the body, the cloth and whatever they touch are considered unclean and must be isolated; similar superstition exists in civilized Europe. Some sailors believe while on board the ship when a woman who has her period stands next to the sailor the gyroscope does not function properly[11].

Influence of monotheistic religions

The conclusion can be drawn from this chapter that heavenly and mono-theistic religions have been instrumental for the dawn of advanced civilization in humankind; they have rescued people from ignorance and dark days and have described and confined the rights and limitations for man and woman within (the framework of) reasoning and logic. In particular, they have delivered woman, this fine and elegant creation, from carrying so much pain and torment from the past; they have laid the groundwork for her achieving freedom and they have restored her inherent gifts entrusted by the charity of nature.

It is incumbent on humanity, specially woman, to be thankful for services of Messengers of God and the wholesome efforts that great thinkers and reformers of the world have made in reawakening "the way" of the creation. They should forever be indebted to these magnanimous heavenly men and men of significance; appreciate the greatness of their souls and minds as well as their sincerity of belief and purity.

CHAPTER TEN
Qualitative evolution of woman's status, worldwide

Schiller, the famed German poet and philosopher says: "Waiting for philosophers and thinkers to govern the world with clear mind, in the meantime, our hunger and (desire for) lust rule....."

Motivational factors of human

Most definitely the primary and strongest motivation for man's advancement has been hunger. This active factor has been operational since humans came into existence to which most of human's achievements are attributed. Historical testimonies show that humankind has never ceased to satisfy this natural need. How many geographic expeditions, bloody conquests and slaughters have been observed to be instigated by this sense. Human's primitive innovations such as hunting, fishing, farming as well as modern industrial and social developments are all attributed to this requirement.

Hunger

Primitive man similar to civilized man was forced to apply most of his faculties towards meeting hunger to fill his belly. Upon entering socialized life, he would have to apply even more effort to satisfy his hunger since living alone and with no disturbances by others, he was only confronting natural difficulties and obstacles; but now in the midst of society, in addition to the routine struggle he would have to defend his interests and confront, and sometimes, fight with people who have opposing ideas in order to have access to natural resources and means of living. On the other hand, he is aware that if he decides to live as an individual within society, his resources alone would not be sufficient to earn him a living and defend him against inconvenience; he would have more success in achieving his goals with the protection and cooperation of others. That is because special relationships with others such as closeness, friendship, cooperation and profit sharing within the cooperative will allow him to enlist partners and assistants to overcome natural difficulties and inconveniences of outsiders.

Based on this observation the need to satisfy hunger has been instrumental in the creation of societies, industries and social institutes as well as other impressions and manifestations of humanity.

Inconvenience and special skills

Upon transition of humankind from solitary to communal life, the prevalent conflict, friction and annoyance among the tribes and groups gave way to cooperation and assistance, to a certain extent, through cooperations of societies with each other. In reality, however, the inherent sources of conflict, notably hunger, became intensified. In fact they were replaced by more complex and fundamental conflicts, such as poverty, itself the source of hunger in societies. The intensity and sharpness of this battle varies according to sphere of influence and the strength of societies. The most horrendous of all wars took place between two most powerful nations. As man became more socially engaged, reproduction increased and societies expanded; subsequently, their expectations and needs increased on a daily basis, demanding more consumer goods. To acquire these goods, or to manufacture them from raw materials, more difficulties and natural obstacles were encountered. Societies, in turn, responded by strengthening their state of intellectual ability to resist and fight against new challenges, environmental and any other inconveniences.

Societies encountering such obstacles produce powerful and creative people who are singled out from ordinary ones. These individuals will achieve distinguished and valuable skill; who are privileged with distinction because of their multi-faceted manifestation of human strength. Inevitably, the use of their superior physical and intellectual capacity over others will equip such societies with new power and strengthen their body structure and brain cells. They are then allowed to take command of the fate of others and as a result they rule over others.

Lust

Pleasure or longing for reproduction? As mentioned before, mankind is born with a sense of an unconditioned need to maintain a full belly in order to satisfy hunger. Immediately after the first need for nourishment, in the order of enticements, man immediately would feel the need for lust. This effective and natural urge is considered, similar to the first stimulant, one of the animalistic as well as humanistic characteristics of primitive societies.

Distinction of senses

The difference between the intensity and effect of these two senses is that hunger is the requirement for maintaining individual life while lust is the means for continuity and durability of a kind of life. Hunger results from greed for individual and personal durability without which man cannot survive because nutrition is the requirement for being alive. Lust, however, results from physical and instinctive human affection for prototyping, with reproduction as its goal. Therefore it is not humanly possible to defy and defeat hunger, but it is possible to harness the sense of lust as practiced by monk abstinence and. By doing so, however, the typical life of human will be vulnerable.

Therefore, from the viewpoint of social and typical life, the effective outcome of these two feelings are the same. In any case as the German thinker, Schiller has stated all the manifestations of human and animal lives have come to exist in various forms, ruled by these two powerful agents.

Lust among animals
Among the relatively more distinguished animals, satisfying lust requires partnership of male and female in a gathering to last for a while. These gatherings are often temporary and at most lasts until such time necessary for nurturing the newborn. No matter how short the period of this gathering may be both parties are bound to show regard for one another. Managing of this joint-life forces the male animal to acquire the consent of female animal to a certain extent. From this mutually beneficial partnership, especially their natural inclinations in caring for their newborn and older children, affectionate feelings as well as ethical and human-like social customs may be developed.

Lust among humankind
The manner just described demonstrates the process of animals sharing their lives. What about humankind? Primitive man was not much different from the archetype of advanced class of animals. All their feelings and affections were also exhibited, at a weaker level, by various kinds of animals.

The correct meaning of "worldly" love, which is lust, exits equally for human and animal. Love is also manifested, in certain class of animals, accompanied by courtesy and feelings which would make it more poetic and more sensitive to feelings than the savage tribes of humankind. Most animals conceal the quality of satisfying their lust with poetic adornment. Pure spiritual love and heavenly attachments that occupied poets and artists thoughts, were unknown and foreign to animals; interestingly, they equally appeared vague and irrational to a majority of members of the human race.

Lovemaking among animals

Nightingale tries to attract his female counterpart with favor and charming song, peacock attempts to hypnotize peahen eyes with charming colors and designs of its feathers and wings. For some special types of birds, in the southern hemisphere, the male and female connect their beaks, moving their heads in harmony with a rhythmic tune and stare at each other for some time. A special bird[1] in the southern region of Americas, builds a bird nest for marriage which could truly be called a bridal chamber. Inside the nest flowers and soft colored weeds are spread out like velvet and in order to avoid all green monotony he tries to beautify the place with laying multi-color flowers, small crystal type pebbles, seashells and ear shell, etc. More amazing is his replacing the stale flowers with new ones. These bird nests are built so strong that they can last for successive generations[2].

Definitely, humans, with harsh and primitive minds belonging to savage tribes and nomads in Africa and South Pacific, and suffering from stupidity, would be incapable of appreciating so many of these fine accomplishments of bird (animals).

Modesty among primitive men

Among the uncivilized men and even those relatively close to the civilization, just like the primitive man, the sense of shame and ignominy is absolutely non-existent. An Australian Aborigine woman (or a native American in southern region of North America) with no decency or modesty is completely naked and except in cold weather she does not cover herself. In studying the status and conditions of these tribes it becomes apparent that primitive men like animals had no inhibition or feeling of shame in expressing their sexual desires. The sense of modesty and decency first appeared among women, strengthened by man's jealousy and his desire to chase women. It should be noted that decency as practiced by ancient tribes is relative with respect to peculiarity and the lineage of the tribe. For example, in the Tahiti islands, ethical necessity is that women be naked from waist down. In China, decency requires that women do not show their legs to men. Also, in conversations, mentioning a woman's leg is indecent. Even the skilled Chinese painters refrain from showing a woman's leg in a picture.

In Japan until early 20th century, the poor families would rent their daughters for a specified period in order to provide dowry for them. This rental could be arranged with a specified person or to a brothel house and in any case at the date of expiry of contract, upon fetching the necessary funds, the woman would be free and a candidate for marriage. Her shameful past would have no negative effect on her social status at all; neither would it harm her possible marriage which could be easily arranged.

Considering the variety and contradiction of customs, it is clear that primitive man was obedient to, and defeated by, the two senses of hunger and lust. Further, a sense of modesty and shame was not a natural tendency of man before certain feelings derived from culture and advanced nurturing, similar to other moral values, influenced man's behavioral thinking. The intensity, weakness and circumstances associated with these changes depended on the level of intellectual and mental growth of individuals. It is conceivable that under certain circumstances such as certain kind of disease and danger of death, this sense of modesty and shame was erased from the conscience of man and even woman and, as such, it was ultimately defeated and destroyed by the excitement of lust.

Woman as perceived by primitive man: The first period

Since in this (ancient) period woman was nothing but a tool for man's pleasure, and unable to defend herself from man's aggression and invasion and because men had no other thoughts than having a filled belly and a never-ending desire for lust, the strongest of them, would keep as many women as he wished. Furthermore, since men believed women did not possess the same soul, mind and feelings (as they did) she neither had the rights to consider herself as partner of man, nor was she allowed to express her jealousy when her husband demonstrated his "love" for another woman; and because the woman was a property and an object belonging to man no one was allowed to do any harm to his "thing" which he owned; the woman was, however, not allowed to submit herself to another man without her owner's permission and consent.

In short, man could do anything to his wife, as he would do to any other properties and materials that he owned. He could loan or rent her and allow other men to share his "tool" for pleasure. The relationship of father and daughter, too, followed the same pattern; the father, even though powerful, would not attempt to prevent any advances made to his daughter by other men.

Woman as perceived by virtuous man: The second period

After the salvation of man from idolatry and violence in the second period, woman's life began to improve in relative terms. In this period heavenly laws forever changed the man's process of thinking hence improved his perception and attitude towards women. No longer would woman be treated as soulless and an object to be owned. Religions limited man's choices and provided certain rights for women; man's cruelty and aggressions to women were no longer visible. Although woman was still a tool for man's pleasure, she no longer was treated as a soulless and mindless tool as in the past. Man could not trade her as he wished. Religions forbade mixed marriage to preserve family blood relation. Sons ought not be allowed to ignore their mothers; they were instructed to obey her wishes at all times, for the pleasure of God.

Weak creature

Still, in this second period woman was considered a weak creature and submissive to man in all respects. She was simply hopeless and too weak as opposed to man's physical strength and intellect. She had absolutely no rights to engage in social affairs and outside her own home men still did not recognize any social status for her.

Any physical ownership, or personal choices of owning property were at the discretion of her husband and only to a degree that he would permit. Her worshipping in religious places did not have the same value as that of a man because she was thought to be weak minded and capricious. Her mixing and conversing with men and exiting from the house by herself was prohibited.

Legally and judicially, the woman was not worthy of having a relationship with her father or her son; only natural blood relation was acceptable and this objective could not be achieved without the existence of male child. Daughter could not be qualified as the protector of her father's family lineage because she would eventually marry a man outside of her family. This explains why the worth of son and daughter, translated to man and woman, would be unequal. The root of this thought process originated from the primary basis of social organizations of this period.

Man and woman were still differentiated with respect to the eternity of spirit. In Christianity, and specifically Catholicism in Spain and Italy, after lengthy discussions it was decided that among all women only Mary was a human with eternal spirit and all other women were in a perilous situation between human and animal.

Some societies believed that woman, contrary to man, did not possess an eternal spirit; hence the ruling that the wife should also die when her husband dies; otherwise she must not re-marry. Among some tribes, when a man dies, it is customary that an honorable wife would commit suicide, or would prepare herself to be incinerated alive with him. This act does not originate from woman's feelings or intensity of her love towards her husband, but as an expression of submission to him and her humility. If feelings were instrumental in committing this act it should have been reciprocated by the husband, had his wife died.

Woman, in this period was considered a servant to her husband. The degree of applicability of title "servant" was dependent on environmental conditions and the level of society's education or civility; in extreme cases, the woman's title was reduced to a slave.

To summarize, this period of history, on the one hand, kept women as in the past period in the state of weakness and hopelessness with men in full control. On the other hand, man's feelings and thinking, though influenced by spirituality and moderated somewhat, remained more or less unfavorable. Any poetic and spiritual experiences would still be rare and unprecedented. Man was still focused on satisfying his two natural senses of ravenousness and lust while woman remained a tool for his lust satisfaction. A notable difference emerged as the man became conscious of and concerned with his treatment of the weak and hopeless woman as a result of his newly acquired beliefs.

Woman as perceived by civilized man: The third period

During this period the manner of reflection of man was completely changed and spirituality flourished to its perfection. Religious thoughts and teachings became extremely clear and pure. Piousness offered salvation to mankind from human perdition; and, as its ultimate goal and final objective, freed humankind from confinement in darkness and bigotry due to ignorance and meandering. To achieve this intent, it made a distinction in its teachings, between worldly benefit and loss, goodness and evilness of soul and body, moral soundness and corruption in this world and Hereafter and delivered a harmonious and perfectly prosperous society. The religious teachings taught people that prosperity in the worldly life is contingent upon the goodness of Hereafter and vice versa.

Since religion has placed the reformation of human condition as a popular aspiration and a priority, it has become a source of inspiration for such thoughts even in places where people are non-believers. These thoughts did cause fundamental changes in the social status of tribes living during the Period of Ignorance; so much that many women were rescued from a vortex of submissiveness and contempt to be elevated as equal partner with their husbands.

Delicate being

During the third period, woman became aware of proper nurturing and its effects on her recognized status which, in turn, allowed her to participate in social affairs away from home. This fundamental change led to the development and flourishing of her qualities and potential. These qualities were otherwise hidden in her body and soul. As a result, woman was transformed from the status of weak creature to a delicate being.

During this period, man realized that while a major part of his life was fraught with intolerable difficulties, hardship and struggle to make a living, an equally important part of life, namely, carrying a child, giving birth, nurturing the children and preparing them for confronting these difficulties of every day life, were the contribution and special duty of woman.

Man understood that the advantage of nurturing along with strengthening the foundation of ethical motives of children were owed to mothers right kind of training, encouragement and persuasion towards their acquiring superior morals. Daughters, in this period, instead of being thought of being worthless and "extra" members of family were transformed to delicate being similar to fine pieces of art and were respected and endeared by family members.

Progress in civil societies and advanced teachings, during this period, transformed human's minds and feelings. It replaced violence with a high level of purity and friendship. No longer was the man content with mere satisfaction of hunger and lust; instead he perceived, in himself, a longing for poetic expression of his desire. That after so much of self indulgence, he still has an appetite for lust, is the manifestation *mota-javel* (diabolical) of human soul's perpetual dissatisfaction.

Poetry and language would be needed to interpret nature's secrets by combining them with pure feelings. Viewing beautiful objects and charming sceneries of nature intoxicates the man; aside from body pleasures and animal enjoyment, he is searching for those pleasures without which he feels dissatisfied and fearful:

At nights he is in solitude with stars,
sharing his secrets with them, and
wishing to know of their full-of-riddles secrets.
But I know he has a lost soul, and unless he finds it he will not rest.

At this time the Wise men named Hafiz, Saadi, Rumi, Nezami, Khayyam, Schiller, Goethe, Shakespeare and Victor Hugo all appear (in front of him) and speak to him of his lost love:

"For years, her heart had wished jame-jam from us;
what she already had, she wanted from the strangers.
The gemstone that was out of the natural(creation) shell;
searched for the lost souls from the sea side.

I complained to every group of people;
I paired with happy ones and unhappy ones.
Everyone in his own thought, became my companion;
in me, he could not find my secrets.
My secret is not far from my complaint;
but this light has no eyes and ears. "

Interpretation:
"They have seen a lover sitting with a group of people, not able to speak about his beloved with the strangers. One of the guests in the

group recites a poem describing all the qualities of the beloved. What an ecstasy and joy; what a deliberation and uproar were found in the lover's soul."

Precisely the words of the poem for a man who does not know where his beloved is and how to express her qualities (attributes) and where are fellow-sufferers, to hear his bereaved soul, having the same effect. They seem to be aware of his soul speaking to him with the language of his heart.

Alas such person no longer imagines the woman as a tool for his physical pleasure. Woman in his view is a beautiful being and piece of art whose face is an impression of signs of the beauty of creation. Not only is he mindful of woman and not only does he respect her, but he would endear her like a fine piece of art. Man, for everything and at any time, gives priority to woman and respects her wishes.

The Prophet of Islam kissed his honorable daughter's hand and kneeled for his wife when she mounted the horse and begged *Aiesheh* to speak to him when he was despondent to stimulate his mind. He took advantage of women's discussions and partnered with them in all social affairs.

To sum up, woman, in this period, is equal and of the same rank with man; she is entitled to all of man's rights and if she does not involve herself in some, it is not due to her being regarded as weak or with shortcomings, as in the past, rather it is because of the nature of the job and its required skill, rules of job allocation as well as her exclusive domain of bearing of, and giving birth to, a child that nature has granted the woman.

It is worth noting that the genesis and foundation of improving woman's lot during this period are the teachings of Islam. The new thoughts that have given women equal respect as men, at all social levels, are sourced from the living instructions of Islam. Still (before

1938) French Civil Code considered a married woman a "minor" and in need of man's guardianship. Fourteen hundred years ago, Islam gave women such capability that she would directly manage her own financial affairs.

Here, again, it should be repeated that the great thinkers of humanity with their far reaching foresight should be appreciated and particularly women should thank God for their salvation from hardship and destitution and being awarded the position of respect and living in comfort and tranquility.

Virtue and indecency, inherent and nominal
Goodness and evil are not, according to some, thought to be inherent, but both are relative and acquired. Therefore, progress in a civilization does not necessitate the prior existence of comfort and prosperity. Based on this observation it is not clear if today's society is happier than the vicious and barbaric tribes of yesteryear. The believers of this opinion claim that the tragic situation of women within a primitive tribe, based on their knowledge and thought process as well as expectations, at the time, should be compared with today's women's situation in relative terms.

Jean-Jacques Rousseau, (1712 – 1778), Genevan philosopher, writer, and composer, and his followers observed a lack of clarity as to whether civilization is positively correlated with higher standard of living. Ancient primitive tribes are thought to have lived free from obligation as well as articles of luxury. They were also not bound to obey any laws and complex rules and disciplines. Yet, the existing traces of civilization counters this claim; among the nations, intellectual growth and prosperity do go hand-in-hand. The greater the population of a prosperous civilized country, the more comfortable and serene the living conditions of the nation will become. To date, thousands are nurtured from farm products of one acre of farm land which in the past could hardly meet his own nutritional need.

The supposed freedom of ancient savages is not only unenviable, but it is sorrowful. What is the value of freedom that exposes a man to hunger, extreme cold, wind, storms and the assorted forces of nature while making a man slave to his needs including the barbaric animal-like lust. The greatness and real happiness of man is attributed to his intellectual and reflective faculty. Intellect draws the man towards God and the truth. Real freedom for man is his salvation from imprisonment and slavery of selfishness, sensual desires and self indulgence.

If, however, today's civilized man is a slave to sensual lust or caught in the web of discipline of civilization, so were yesteryear's savages who were definitely slaves to lust and childish desires as well as being imprisoned by nature's cruelties.

It is true that as an example of indecency, in most cases, larceny is condemned by almost everyone. Nevertheless, it is still considered acceptable and fair among some tribes, where a young man would not qualify to become a family's son-in-law because he is not able, or else he refuses to demonstrate his bravery and valor by steeling others' belongings, or being a bandit.

No person can ever prefer the sound of a donkey over a Nightingale song, or not enjoy the scenic view of blue sky with glittering stars, or not having the pleasure of seeing waterfalls and a garden filled with colorful tulips.

An analogy may be drawn as to whether those primitive black men of Africa would not enjoy a pretty plain face of white women with fascinating blue eyes. This, in contrast to viewing an inelegant sight by decorating their faces with large heavy rings, embedded into their lips and nose. Likewise, whether man would recognize the position of expanded intellect versus selfness, virtue versus indecency or goodness versus evil, as being the same.

Any person free of prejudice and suspicion will appreciate (good) deed and fairness, will reject persecution and oppression and would prefer truth to lies. The differences in recognizing deeds as being virtuous or indecent, observable by humankind, are caused by factors such as ego, bad nurturing and wrong habits that interfere in the final outcome which, in turn, would contaminate and confuse man's sense of correct recognition. In other words, generally everyone recognizes the sameness of issues, in broad terms. The discrepancy lies in recognizing and making judgements on specificity and details.

Everyone belonging to the warring parties agree, with a unified voice, on their preference of right over wrong, fairness to oppression and truth to lie. The disagreement and resulting bloodshed stems from the reference which is applied, that is, what statement is the truth and what claim is invalid. Which party is telling the truth and who is going about lying. Since claims of both parties are motivated and tainted with self serving purpose from each party's viewpoint, truth is a lie and lie is the truth. Otherwise, in cases that to a person, with a clear mind and free from any prejudice, virtue and indecency appear the same and similar to other examples.

Based on the above argument, woman's misery and unbearable tragic events in the past, even though some may assume to have been "part of" the customs and habits of the time and therefore understandable and palatable; nevertheless the reality of wretchedness, poverty, suffering and oppression have been bitter and unpalatable. Furthermore, women were denied education and proper nurturing, deprived from achieving desired perfection and happiness. That is why women must be thankful, for the blessing of present day comfort and tranquility. They should take note that as a token of expressing thanks, for blessed freedom, they must demonstrate their meritoriousness and capabilities; otherwise, the way of creation will soon take away the blessings for which one is not worthy.

PART II

Modern women's rights:
Civil and Moral Laws

CHAPTER ONE
Women's rights in marriage

Marriage in the world

As previously described in detail, animals as well as human beings feel sensual after overcoming their hunger. To satisfy this natural need, male and female creatures confront each other with feelings not unlike desires from one another. In ancient human societies, as in some animal gatherings, marriage of male and female, as it is generally perceived, did not exist. Yet they did satisfy themselves by cohabiting as mixed male and female because their purpose for the gathering was to satisfy their lust.

The natural need for lust later on was extended to natural instinct which reflected the love of self, requiring preservation of the kind. This natural instinct, that is, the love of protecting their "prototypes" forced human, as well as some animals, to seek additional means of satisfaction for this new found desire of reproducing well beyond lust. The tool, or means for satisfying this desire of preserving became known as *reproduction*. Reproduction allows the natural instinct to transform itself through the expression of love between male and female creatures where they meet. From this instinctive love an organized, but limited union is then evolved.

Animal union for reproduction

To clarify this topic, one should first briefly consider the grouping, or the animal union. Such mixing of male and female can be interpreted as merely a natural need. The male animal with no effort and expectation of loyalty approaches any female who is available to him and after satisfying his need the couple go their separate ways. A regular gathering, that one can interpret as mixed marriage, results from a natural instinct based on prototyping of the kind. It may initially be perceived that the love of reproducing, the burden of child bearing and expression of affection towards them would contradict the nature of selfishness and self adulation. One must therefore explore the origin of the desire for reproduction. It follows that the love of making a prototype of self is another manifestation of selfishness and self appreciation. Hence no contradiction. The animal whose reproduction is based on dissemination[1] of newborn is exactly a copy of, and part of, the parents. This is true whether a creature lays an egg or gives birth to a newborn copy.

At any event, from the love of reproducing to maintaining and nurturing offspring, a regular and permanent, or at least lengthy, association is developed. Such a lengthy period is normally a function of the time needed for offsprings to be sufficiently developed; that is, being able to protect themselves from dangers and independently nourish themselves. Afterwards the union of animals will dissolve; they separate and become strangers to one another.

Within a group of animals, where the female is a majority, polygamy is the rule. Roosters, for example, keep several hens under their control and jealously protect them against competitors. Multiple husbands among animals is rare because the female animal is weaker and is already controlled by the 4male; furthermore, she can never approach another male against the wishes of her male partner.

There is an affinity and respect towards the strongest male animal among the females. During a fight over a female animal involving several competing male animals, the female patiently waits for the winner to submit herself. The rule of one female spouse generally holds for birds as well as four-legged animals. This rule applies also to animals experiencing food shortage, dictated by their habitat, and are scattered in various types. It is possible that other as yet unknown factors influence this rule.

One type of monkeys in India will stay with one female partner and always remain faithful to her until death. Also, the male pheasant, turkey and peacock are content with one female partner irrespective of abundance of female species. Also, elephant's loyalty to his female partner is legendary.

In some cases, changes in animals' life style affect the behavior of their married life. For example, a male wild duck that normally stays with one female, after being domesticated, could choose many female partners. In other cases, animals' sole partnership and their mutual loyalty turns into extremely ethical and noticeably noble behavior. They may be so touched, saddened and depressed, sometimes permanently, as the result of their loss of the spouse. This is far less observed in surviving humans. A special female parrot in Springfield, Illinois, upon the loss of her male partner stops eating until she dies. A similar sacrifice which has been observed is exhibited by a monkey in the Paris Zoo[2].

The difference between animal and human feelings can be explained as lack of direct relationship between feeling and love on the one hand and intellect and intelligence on the other hand. Contrary to animals, humankind recognizes the relationship between "feelings and love" versus intellect. Interestingly enough, there is an inverse relationship between these two. This should explain why, in some cases, man turns out to be harsher than animal.

In short the law that governs the need for instituting and maintaining a married life among animals is an efficient law that can reproduce and ensure its comfort comprising selection, natural habit and instinct.

Marriage as practiced

Marriages among humans is also subject to the law of supply and demand. Initially the motive or purpose for lust did not exist, nor was there a legislated law to protect morality and the weak. Marriage in every tribe or group of people began as mixed marriage. This was in accordance with laws of the land, and the particulars of an environment as well as the ratio of gender. Another factor that contributed to mixed marriage was, the everyday chores for providing food. Later the instinct to reproduce evolved to a regular and legitimate union of one man and one woman, popularly known as marriage.

Since many varied factors and causes, among tribes and groups have influenced the formation of different types of marriage, it may not be possible to look for an evolutionary trend, or to assume that there has been a consistent and unified improvement or an evolution on all fronts. It can, however, be stated that the quality of marriage has evolved relative to social growth and intellect among various nations and tribes, that is, from primitive mixed marriage to a formalized legal and legitimate one. Below is a list of various types of marriage practiced among various tribes and societies.

1. Marriage, outside the family[3]

Some ancient civilizations such as Chinese and Indian, as well as many of primitive tribes believed that no marriage would be allowed within the family belonging to the same tribe. According to this custom, the man and woman must have different roots. The level of intensity of this belief fluctuated between those who accepted marriage of a couple beyond the sixth generation and others who absolutely prohibited any marriage of any generation of the family or tribe. For the case of prohibiting inter-tribe marriage the rationale was based on the fact that tribes were collection of families and to marry outside the family implied outside the tribe. Hence the objection to marry a member of tribe. The outside marriages were of three types.

a. A suitor asking for the hand of a young woman, is usually introduced by a family member and is accepted by the woman's family. The agreement is followed by an exchange of money or gifts offered by the bridegroom for transitioning woman from her father's family to his own.

b. If the suitor's request is rejected by the woman's family and or the bride personally objects (which could be artificial) then the bridegroom, assisted by his friends, will successfully "kidnap" the bride despite any and all objections.

c. A man without any prior request may target and kidnap a woman as a "prisoner" against her will and without any notice to her family.

Cases (b) and (c) specifically take place among those tribes who are committed to avoiding marriage within their own tribe. Case (a) occurs in inter-tribe marriages as well as outside the tribe.

In Tasmania, Australia until recently[4] the custom of marriage has been that a man would ambush a woman from another tribe who was away from her turf and alone; then by striking her with a wooden stick hard enough for her to become unconscious, he would drag her to a temporary place away from her tribe. Upon regaining her senses and sufficiently rested, he would command her to follow him to his home and become his wife. Afterwards the men from both tribes would meet to settle the affair by arranging a mock attack by the youth representing the bride's tribe complete with bow and arrow and a protective shield against the bridegroom's tribe. The bridegroom would fully shield himself, while the attacker would refrain from targeting him. A few minutes later the show is over and peace and tranquility return. Finally, the bride-groom's tribe would invite the bride's family to a feast; often, to seal the peace pact. The events end by tying both bride and bridegroom to a tree, breaking one tooth from each. The woman would then be considered the legitimate wife of the man and he is allowed to deal with her in any fashion he pleased.

Apparently the above style of artificial kidnapping is a mild version of real forced kidnapping. In any case since this type of marriage along with tradition and ceremonies are not convenient, Australian men would prefer instead to have primitive mixed marriage to satisfy their sexual desire; or for a fee rent or borrows their friends' wives for a specified time.

On the other hand, it is noted that marriage of this kind, not only nominally, but in reality, had deviated from its original intent. It had basically aban-doned the intent and the meaning of marriage. This version of marriage, by implication, no longer assumes to be a means for satisfying human need and reproducing; rather it is reduced to a criminal and immoral act of kidnapping women. This kind of marriage ultimately degrades women to the level of a four-legged animal for the purpose of carrying heavy loads as well as hard labor chores carried out under harsh conditions; all this in addition to being responsible for feeding her family and minding the children. A family resulting from this kind of marriage is naturally leader-less. The mother has lost all her dignity, personality and authority and her children cannot be expected to be nurtured and guided by her.

Another type of abusing the act of marriage is to allow boys and girls to mix together and indulge in any act to satisfy their lust. Girls from the age of ten would be allowed to associate with boys as young as four-teen. The parents even celebrated when their daughters enjoyed mixing together.

Since the purpose of marriage had turned out to be a working arrange-ment, women under thirty years old were rarely captured or imprisoned.

Additionally, mixed marriage by itself was a cause for woman infertility, leading to drastic reduction of offsprings seeds. This coupled with rising suicide among women, caused the tribe's female population to contract which, in turn, encouraged more of mixed marriage with other tribes outside their surroundings.

The higher echelon and rich people of the tribe had a number of women under their control. Usually a man could have three to four legitimate wives reserved for the husband and the rest he could offer to his foot soldiers and favored servants to demonstrate their goodwill and strengthen their sense of loyalty and service. Inheritance was reserved especially for male children, and only of his legitimate wives.

These legitimate wives had other duties towards their husband which are still in effect in some parts of the world. In Fuji/*Tonga* islands a woman, in the beginning of her married life, had to search for a young girl, adopt her as her own daughter and nurture her. Upon her reaching adolescence, and about the same time that the wife reached the age of her maturity, one morning after bathing the girl and making her presentable she led her to her husband's chamber completely undressed. Satisfied that mission is accomplished, she then quietly walked away leaving them alone.

When the couples are married from two different tribes, neither one can speak the language of the other. Any warmth and affection between the wife and husband are rare and hard to find, so much so that after several years of living together neither one has shown any interest in learning the other's language. They use sign language pointing to each other as means of communication.

2. Marriage within the family[5]
In contrast to previous type of marriage, some nations and tribes, whether civilized or primitive, were committed to marriages taking place among their own relatives and, at the very least, within their own tribe or group

of people. Among the civilized nations of Iran and Egypt the rationale for this view was to maintain the status of blood purity and nobility. As mentioned in chapter six (Part 1) ancient Iranians considered blood purity and continuity of family generation quite important and fearing that mixed blood would cause blood contamination and lowering of morals, they legitimized incestuous marriage. Ancient Egyptians often married their sisters. Most Egyptian queens were proud to be the sister and wife of the king.

In Peru, the inside the family marriage was also prevalent in the past. At first only the Inca king was allowed to marry his sister, provided she had a different mother than the king. Later the tribal chiefs and other leaders were also allowed to practice this type of marriage. Among the primitive tribes practicing inside (the family marriage was mostly due to poverty of tribal members) as an inexpensive marriage.

Generally, habits and customs that later were compiled as the "book of law" follow the natural needs of community and are derived from environmental particulars of a tribe. Even the public behavior of a tribe follows the same kind of needs. Study of the tribes living conditions will show that the prevalence of either external or internal marriage in a tribe is the compatibility of either type with the tribe's needs based on their natural conditions and circumstances. For example, in less populated tribes external marriage and in more populous tribes normally internal marriages are common. Within those tribes where female population is high, polygamy is prevalent.

The members of families who marry outside their family do a better job in reinforcing their race and purity of genesis. This is based on the law of nature applied to vegetation and animals. It is well known that mixed and unrelated textures improve growth. Marriage within the family, though it gives the appearance that it protects the purity of blood and prevents its mixing with a lower grade blood, in reality and based on the above-mentioned laws of nature, it would lead to diminution and decline of the offspring. That is why in today's civil laws of the many civilized countries, marriage within a family is both unlawful and morally bankrupt. *Omar-Ibn-L-Khattab*, when passing by a tribe, noted the people were all weak with yellow skins. It turned out that the members of tribe only married within the tribe. Omar advised them to marry people from other tribes and quoted from the Prophet, *"marry an expatriate"*.

Herbert Spencer believed that external marriage that required kidnapping the bride was popular among hostile tribes; conversely, the pacified and peace-loving tribes opted for internal marriage. An unusual and exceptional tribe in New Zealand was the most hostile one in South Pacific area; they married both within their tribes and their family as well as outside their tribe. *Lennon*, a social scientist thought that kidnapping the women and taking them as prisoner were the characteristics of external marriage, but the above-mentioned tribe in New Zealand did just that even when married within their own tribe or to their relatives. As noted before, this idea of kidnapping of woman, externally or internally, was intended to prove man's manhood ability and capability of the woman's family. In their minds a man who did not have such power did not deserve to marry.

Polygamy (plurality of female spouses)-There are certain different causes and factors that create polygamy. Increased ratio of females to males within the society is the first condition. It can be said that in a society where there are more women than men, any prohibition of polygamy necessarily results in promotion and increase in prostitution because, aside from earning for livelihood, undoubtedly women are not immune to their need for company of men. Accordingly, unmarried women will naturally gravitate towards prostitution. At any event, the choice and advantages, or faults of this matter is a separate subject of debate. Generally, in places where there are more women than men polygamy is permissible, but since maintenance of several women requires extra financial means this type of marriage is reserved for the wealthy and well to do people.

Islam has made polygamy permissible contingent upon the man's financial status as well as man's observing justice and compassion for his wives; otherwise it is prohibited. Even the possibility that the man may not be able to act with justice between his women would suffice to deny him permission to marry. Justice and compassion between two women means that the man must extend equal love for both wives which is difficult if not undoable.

Among some tribe polygamy is allowed if the woman is sterile. Among some African tribes[6] polygamy is permitted, embraced and appreciated by both men and women. Except among Christian nations, in other parts of the world polygamy is permissible.

The Christian missionaries have encountered difficulties in promoting their religious teachings on the subject of polygamy with little success to report. This is partly because women themselves are receptive to this type of marriage. Noting that in that part of the world(Africa), the burden of daily living rests with women and they naturally want to share their hardship with others. Naturally, the more women introduced to work force the lesser will be the hardship. They even encourage their husbands to marry younger women since a junior wife will obey her and moreover the younger she is the harder she works; additionally, since the husband hardly would express any affection to his wife there was no cause for jealousy among the women.

4. Uni-spouse

This kind of marriage is current in advanced and economically developed countries as well as most Christian nations. It is the best and most proper kind of marriage when there is no excess of female population. In some primitive tribes due to excessive weakness of mental faculty and physical fitness coupled with poverty and destitution this type of marriage is the only choice. For example, among the people of *Weddal* of Sri Lanka and India, or Islands of *Lou-Tcbou* near China where most women lived in captivity under wretched conditions; they fully obey their husbands, and men never take another woman[7].

5. Polygamy (plurality of male spouse): Zamad[8] marriage

Two important contributors cause a strange and unnatural type of marriage. One is numerical shortage of woman population in a particular region; another is man's debased and bankrupt level of thought process and feelings. These two factors, which are highly correlated, have been instrumental in sharply lowering people's morals in various parts of the world.

The female population of nations is normally not less than males and in fact it is more in certain regions, according to statistical data, both historically and projected. Therefore, decrease in female population is attributed to such vile act as murdering of daughters (in places such as Arabia during the Period of Ignorance) or epidemics of abortion, or promoting prostitution and mixing of man and woman which would cause woman's infertility. All such immoral acts, in turn, interrupted the natural process of re-production which affects the balance in distribution of sexes.

This kind of polygamy is more like the kind of mixed and disordered marriage which was exercised in the early days of formation of human communities and is apparently a continuation of that chaos. Undoubtedly, in the past, instead of the legal marriage practiced in most societies there were primitive and pre-historic communities engaged in purely mixed sexual and lustful activities.

In New Caledonia, outside-the family marriage is prevalent while the practice of inside-the family marriage is prohibited, but the prohibition only applies to the maternal side of the family. This indicates that based on the background, as well as the effects of an ancient mixed marriage, correct identification of a child's father is difficult hence only the mother is identified. The *Andamanites* Islands[9] woman belonged to all the family members when she married a man of the family. If she resisted advances made by any "important" man in the family it was considered a major sin for which she, the guilty one, was punished.

The women of *Naires* tribe usually took five to six husbands; she was ultimately allowed to increase the number to twelve husbands. She lived for ten days with each husband and each husband could, in turn, be attached to a few wives, spending several days with each of them. For the people of these tribes, and particularly the Himalayans, polygamy for a woman was not shameful at all and did not damage woman's social prestige. For example, among people of *Nepauls,* a lie even if minor, was considered quite repugnant, but polygamy of women was morally acceptable.

As for recognition and division of children the arrangement was simple. The oldest child will belong to oldest husband and the rest were identified and distributed according to their age as compared to presumed father's age. In Arabia the wife had to suggest a child that would most likely resembled the potential father. In the event that all fathers rejected the choice the child would take the mother's name.

6. Acquired marriage

In most civilized countries from ancient days until not long ago, and among most primitive tribes even now, a woman is treated as physical merchandise sold by her father. In ancient Rome and Greece, as discussed before, exchanging a woman was a routine and typical marriage.

In general, no explanation was needed when the type of marriage was found to be directly related to the worth and social status of the woman in that society. To the extent that the status of women has improved in most societies, the procedure of marriage was also refined and amended with more attention to women's rights. The following examples demonstrate the point.

Men of primitive tribes sold their daughters based on their monetary value. The agreed price was then established as their dowry. Later, however, since man and wife were considered partners for life with equal rights in everything the matter of purchase and payment became moot.

The African tribe *Hottentos* would exchange a woman for several Oxen. The younger the woman, the more valuable she was since in a hot and humid environment, the girls reached puberty sooner and likewise their energy was depleted faster as they aged. Because the marriage was a trade this could be cancelled or offset, with mutual consent.

Among the *Coffres* tribesmen, if the buyer paid the total amount of the purchase price the woman's father would relinquish his ownership rights of his granddaughters; otherwise an equivalent of the uncollected amount could be reclaimed by him, regaining the ownership of his granddaughters, This allowed him to offer his grandchildren for sale to the higher bidder.

The *Solima* tribe allowed a woman to return the money she had received to her husband and marry another man. In the case that the couple had children the woman had to additionally compensate her husband for the hardship of their birth as practiced by *Guinea* tribe.

The *Kourango* tribe would not allow a woman to be sold more than once. After divorce, and her freedom from her husband she would be the sole owner of herself and free. Old men purchased young women and after their death, the women were free to remarry.

Purchasing a woman by African tribesmen required a pre-paid purchase price for which the woman had to work as long as she could endure. Since there has never been a moral cause, duty or motive for the husband to help his wife this case had no relevance except in those places where woman was no longer able to work effectively. An African (man) told a European explorer, "since I have bought her she must work for me like an ox".

Among some Saharan tribes a young woman is forced to work as a prostitute to earn her family's subsistence; later on when she is sold (through marriage) she would be free from her obligation and whatever she receives from her husband would be hers alone.

In some places, if the husband is unable to pay his way for taking a wife he must pay to the family of his wife an equivalent free labor. Moses shepherded for marrying Sarah for many years. So did Jacob for marrying Rachelle. In Africa, after a man is endowed with a daughter, his father-in-law will no longer benefit from his son-in-law. The rationale is that the young daughter will be wedded to her cousin on her maternal side for free and as a result, the wife's family will be able to repurchase the girl without payment to her father.

Among the *Polynesians* when a family's daughter is married, the bride's father, or brother, informs the bridegroom of his right of ownership of his wife-to-be and accordingly he will become her new owner and master. If dissatisfied with the marriage he will be free to sell her, kill her or eat her[10]. In the event the father believes he is short changed he could, within a certain period, take back his daughter and resell her to another buyer at a higher price.

In *Sumatra*, in contrast to other parts of South Pacific, a bride's family pays a man a lump sum amount and would accept him as a bridegroom for their daughter, living with the family. In this case, the husband would be considered the employee of the bride's family and would work according to their business relationship. Any children and earnings that may result from this union would belong to the wife, although this type of arrangement is rare.

The purchase of the wife by a husband, on the other hand, is the most common practice in *Sumatra*. In this type of marriage there are two specific characteristics, both derived from the forceful and natural right of ownership.

First, monetary benefit from woman either by her working, or by making any transaction as the man (father) would consider fair with respect to her situation: such as renting her, loaning her, replacing her or selling her. This is identical to any transactions that one would execute with respect to a physical merchandise.

Second, it prevented others to transgress the man's right of ownership. While the wife can interact with another man upon the recommendation and direction of her husband, her committing to any association with a man without the permission and consent of her husband carried an extreme punishment. This was not because of jealousy, zeal or honor since the understanding of these terms, perhaps, was unknown to most of these people; it was because the man's ownership was invaded. In New Caledonia an adulteress, according to the committee of the elders, was immediately executed.

In Africa, the *Achantis* tribe members may decide to cut the nose of an adulteress and marry her to a slave instead of murdering her. If the wife divulged her husband's secret her upper lip would have been cut-off. If she eavesdropped on the secret conversation of her husband with others they would have cut off her ear. If the husband was absent for three years she could have remarried, but upon the first husband's return the wife and children, including the newborns, would have belonged to him.

The Brahmins would throw both adulteress and her guilty partner in front of wild dogs. That is when the guilty man is Brahman; otherwise they undress the man and make him lie on a red hot iron board.

These extreme punishments were all the result of the basic right of man's ownership of his purchased woman with marriage as its most common and routine manifestation. These customs were practiced even among Aryans and relatively civilized tribes such as Germans, Franks and Slaves. Later Germans decided to replace the purchase price of the agreed amount to dowry, in the form of a gift directly to her. This appeared to be owned by the woman, but in reality it belonged to her father. On the eve of the wedding an amount known as *Osculum*, or *Oseles* as down payment was made for the first kiss, followed by a gift, *Morgengale*, to the bride the morning after.

7. Inherited marriage

This type of marriage is also one of the consequences of the rights of man to own his wife. In Gabon, Africa after the death of a husband, his wife or wives were included in his inheritance and his wealth was distributed among the inheritors. The inheritor would have a choice of the woman for personal use or transferring her to his distant relatives. The *Yaribas* tribe of Africa also would permit the son to inherit the widowed wife of his father and sleep with her, but if she was his own mother he could only make her work with chores such as carrying loads of goods. In Arabia (of Period of Ignorance), the inheritor would cover the wife's body of the deceased wife with his clothes, thereby claiming her as his "inheritance". Such inheritor would then have full rights of ownership of the widowed woman. If she was not his own mother he could marry her without any dowry or marry her to another man, but claim her dowry for himself. He could also forbid her to re-marry. Islam Sharia cancelled this method of inheritance and outlawed such unjust marriages[11].

8. Compulsory and forcible marriage

This kind of marriage, as the words indicate, is another reflection of woman's weakness and despair against man; whether the marriage is executed in the form of purchase and sale or kidnapping or another form. For many centuries, poverty and destitution had forced young women to obey their father's or guardian's decision in selecting a husband and even surrendering against their will. The manifestation of such compulsion and adversity in past periods and in many parts of the world have been observed as primitive or civilized.

Among various European and Aryan tribes during the period of social system of feudalism young women had to formally request marriage permission from their father, master and even the king. Often, the master would reject the husband nominated by her and or her family forcing her to marry his hand- picked husband.

Among the Jews as well as many tribes throughout the world a type of marriage, was practiced commonly known as *Levitate*, and is still being practiced. *Levitate* required that the man must marry his deceased brother's widow, whether he is married or single. Any age appropriateness would be ignored and the lack of inclination of either or both parties would also be disregarded.

In Ancient Iran, as discussed in chapter six of Part I (Ideal Marriage), if the deceased has not left a son the wife or daughter of the deceased would be required to marry the nearest relative on her father's side or her husband's side.

In Ancient Greece, there also existed a similar compulsory rule for the daughter of the deceased to marry a relative of the deceased family that her father would have inherited if she wanted to take advantage of her father's inheritance.

Many Native American tribes such as the *Black Feet, Osages, Cheyennes, Iowas, Kawes, Crease, Crows and Mintari's* consider younger sisters of a man's wife as "compulsory and forcible" wives of that man sharing equal rights, with the official wife, and to all the children in the family. The distress and constraints gradually eased along with continued improvement in women's rights and was even recently incorporated in the civil codes of western nations, as exhortation, admonition and consultation.

In the past a woman was not considered to have an opinion in selecting her husband that would be worth taking into account and basically was a piece of merchandise, or an item of exchange between the parties (her father and the bridegroom). A French world traveler, during his long stay in China observed that Chinese girls can not even conceive of the possibility of being asked their opinion, but in gradual stages woman is becoming a party to transactions and must independently show her desire to marry the other party.

Intervention of parents and guardians is based on the view that they are older and more experienced, hence naturally they are interested in their daughter's goodwill and happiness. It is better if the girl consults with them regarding this serious matter and embrace their advice.

The Civil Code of France has determined the age of twenty-one years as the legally accepted age of adulthood for both sexes. For the purpose of marriage alone, however, a fifteen year old girl and an eighteen year old boy are allowed to marry. Marriage under these age limits other than exceptional cases and with the permission of the President of the Republic is not possible. Couples that are younger than the legal age of twenty-one must obtain their respective parents permission and in their absence, their grand parents. Marriage is not allowed to take place without their consent. For couples aged between twenty-one and twenty five, in the case of absence of parents consent, the couple must formally request permission for the subject of marriage by issuing an official declaration of intent. If after the expiration of the allowed period the permission was not granted and no rejection with legitimate cause was received the marriage contract will be executed.

The Iranian civil law[12] also recognizes legal ages fifteen and eighteen years for girls and boys respectively for marriage. For exceptional cases, where family morals necessitate, the local court may consider the proposal submitted by the local prosecutor to lower the legal ages to thirteen and fifteen years respectively. The marriage of a girl between the ages of fifteen and eighteen years (which is also the legal age for all transactions) can only take place if permission of her guardian is secured. After the age of eighteen years, the marriage of a virgin girl is still dependent on her father's or grand father's permission. If either one of the guardians refuse to grant permission without any legitimate cause, the girl will be able to marry her husband by formally presenting him to the Notary office and notify her guardian of the marriage through that office. After fifteen days from the notification date if the girl's guardian cannot or does not provide a legal objection, the marriage is official. Therefore, today, parents' intervention is only for the purpose of consultation and advice. Even if the intervention has its usual negative effect, the girl cannot be forced to marry a man towards whom she shows no interest; they can only prevent her marriage to the man that they do not approve for the good of the family.

9. Official (civil society) marriage

Today, all civilized nations consider marriage an official matter and manage its quality under the supervision and care of the law. That is because it is the foundation of families and therefore the basis of any social structure of every society. Ancient civilizations also paid some attention to this critical affair. For example, by law men from lower classes were prevented from marrying upper class women.

During the 16th century, and before the Spanish intrusion, Peru was ruled by the powerful Inca dynasty. They had already established marriage affair, as an official and public matter so that no marriage could have taken place without the involvement of local government officials. Once a year, people would gather in *Cuzco*, the capital, as well as other major towns where the king himself along with other leaders, the *Curacas,* would conduct marriage ceremonies between the couples who were considered fit. Afterwards, the king would grant modest living quarters and a piece of land to a married young man for farming as a reward in recognition of his voluntary commitment to marriage.

In Mongolia, a married man committing adultery would be fined collectable by the government. This indicates the seriousness of the crime with regards to marriage that Mongols considered as official matter related to public welfare.

10. Privacy of marriage

Contrary to official marriage practiced in most civilized countries, in most of the less civilized and often primitive parts of the world, marriage was considered a private and individual affair and not of concern to the society and its governing body. No particular laws were enacted concerning private marriage. Everyone, in accordance to his desire and wealth, took a wife in (his) peculiar manner. Treatment of the woman depended on morals and family training of the parties as well as the sentiments and feelings of the man.

In contrast to the Peruvian kingdom which was very much involved in marital affairs, the Mexican[13] government proclaimed total dis-engagement from all marriage matters in 1828. A by-product of such freedom of indulgence led to all kinds of unjust, unglamorous and disgraceful affairs, such as loaning and renting women, as practiced among African and South Pacific tribes.

Mexico, parenthetically and contrary to marriage, considers divorce an official matter to which the government pays attention and for which there is a special court to accommodate couples wanting to separate. After the parties presented their case to this court, they were advised by the court to reconcile their differences. If they insisted the court would take no action, indicating that separation was allowed. The court and the law did not condone divorce, but silence implied permission for the couple to separate.

In Tibet, both marriage and divorce are considered personal and private affairs. Marrying a woman and producing many children is considered a difficult matter and shameful. For this reason marriage and subsequent reproduction were activities reserved for the "ordinary" members of the society.

11. Reproductive marriage

In this kind of marriage the husband's intent is purely reproduction for a new generation and a woman only served that purpose. Most tribes engaged in this kind of marriage sought the production of a male child; a woman who did not produce a son was considered infertile. The basis of this thinking had its origin in the government by-class-distinction which made it necessary to preserve the continuation of generation of the family. Many ancient civilizations that considered having a male child as the only way to maintain the family dynasty adopted some strange plans and policies, such as "Ideal" marriage and child adoption, for example practiced routinely among ancient Iranians. This topic of continuity of family generations, in ancient Rome, Greece and India, had religious undertones. The common belief was that having a son was necessary to maintain the ancestors' divinity.

In the case where a husband proved to be sterile, the Brahmans allowed the wife to be impregnated by the husband's brother. A Hindu wife who for eight consecutive years remains sterile or does not produce a male child is divorced. If the husband proved to be at fault he would allow his wife to be impregnated by his brother or the nearest kin once or twice. In China and ancient Greece sterility is a cause for divorce. According to *Herodotus* two of the Spartan kings did just that.

According to the Laws of Hammurabi,[14] the Caledonians and Assyrians legislated a set of comprehensive laws some five hundred years before the Coming of Moses. Accordingly, if the wife was unable to produce a child the husband could divorce her by paying her dowry. The dowry for a "respected" woman was equivalent to nine kilograms of silver and for a divorced woman one kilogram of silver. The wife could opt to stay in the family home without expecting any loyalty or obligations from her husband. Such arrangement, contrary to general rule which prohibits polygamy, would allow the husband to take another woman as a mistress and not as an official wife. Alternatively the sterile wife at her volition could offer her husband a female slave as such Sarah presented *ha-jar* to Abraham. According to Hammurabi law (articles 44 to 46) if the slave produced a child the master was no longer able to sell her[15].

12. Temporary marriage

In order to discourage prostitution in places where the female population exceeds that of men, or for other reasons certain laws have legitimized the natural inclination of both man and woman, by permitting temporary marriages. It is obvious that the purpose of this type of marriage is to satisfy human lust and is not at all concerned with reproduction. It can even be said that temporary marriage contradicts reproduction. Islam religion permits this type of marriage as "concubine", but as in the case of permanent marriage, it has set requirements and after the expiration (of the period of engagement) has imposed *Eddeh* (a waiting period) to prevent mixing of blood relation. Among the Moroccan Jews, the waiting period of this type of marriage varies from three to six months.

13. Permanent marriage

In some civil and religious laws, marriage is recognized as an unbreakable permanent contract; not only is it an unlimited commitment, but it ignores even the possibility of divorce. The basis of this view is the reverence, the honor and the status of this contract which constitute the formation of a family. Yet, restricting the union of man and wife to this type of marriage, if viewed from both duration and the absence of possibility of divorce,(i.e., a lifetime commitment with no possibility of divorce) is impractical as described below.

a) *Absence of possibility of divorce* -For a couple whose moral differences would make their continued living together an intolerable torture, it is necessary to make provisions for special cases within the governing laws for this kind of marriage contract. It is well known that despite the fact that divorce does not exist in Christianity, under certain conditions, divorce is granted to Christians, sometime over the objection of the Church.

b) *Durability of marriage*- Undoubtedly woman's prestige is well served in the permanency of the marriage; it guarantees that the wife is not to be used, or thought, as a mere tool for pleasure. It should, however, be noted that the natural inclination of man and woman under certain circumstances may lead to improper temporary relationships that would be considered illegitimate relationships and even prostitution (in the absence of a legitimate temporary marriage discussed above).

It is obvious that the illegitimate relationship which is temporary and has no purpose other than satisfying lust, will rock the social and moral position of the wife many times harder than a legitimate temporary marriage. A temporary marriage provides the same temporary inclination and relationship with a legal cover and furthermore disciplines the relationship from the perspective of rights and obligations of the parties. It also prevents mixed parental liability(in case of an illegitimate child).

Of course, in an ideal society where morality, ethics and humanity would deter people from violating the rules of virtue and morals, marriage must only take the form of permanency. Unfortunately the existence of such society cannot even be imagined; it is only an illusion.

14. Experimental marriage

This type of marriage appears to be similar to those of inferior quality and a remnant of the societies whose civilizations are or have been in a permanent decline. It is a direct result of inferior status and destitution of their women in conjunction with the absence of government and civilian attention in the matter of marriage. A typical example of this type of marriage was practiced in Sri Lanka (Ceylon) not long ago.

A marriage contract was kept in a "hold" position until fifteen days had elapsed. If at the end of the 15th day of cohabitation between the spouses the woman was acceptable to man the marriage contract would be confirmed; otherwise the marriage would be cancelled. Obviously, the true intent of this marriage, to an outsider, appeared to be nothing but to buy a young woman (by a man) and selling of the same (by her guardian). The woman had to offer her body to a man as buyer with maximum ease and at the cheapest price until such time that he decided to like and to accept her and, finally, to purchase her; otherwise she had to offer herself to the next buyer[16] at an even lower price.

15. Shared and family marriage

Primitive tribes, as noted before, possess all the elements that promote further ethical and moral degradation. On the one hand, their purpose for marrying is simply to satisfy their animal-like lust and self indulgence. On the other hand, poverty and inability to provide sustenance discourages the young men from marrying and forming families. As a result, in such societies various, albeit invalid and defective types of so-called marriages are practiced. Among Native Americans, especially those living around the California area late in the 19th century, a woman who was initially married to one man in a family would later be shared by all other men in that family; even relationships with men of other families within the tribe was acceptable. A man's jealousy was only aroused if the relationship involved another man in a different tribe. Among the members of *Cingalais* tribe who live in Sri-Lanka, a married woman to one man in the family was essentially considered the property of the family. Basically the man did not marry a woman, but the entire family married a woman.

In Tibet, as noted before, marriage is difficult and also shameful; because of that, family members share this affair to reduce the burden on the individual. So, the senior brother marries one woman for all the brothers. The children of this marriage will all belong to the senior brother. In Nepal, the brothers of one family also purchase one woman as a common commodity at a value of 12-15 rupees and once in a while would even rent her. The children born from all would be distributed in order of age and seniority.

16. Multi- tier marriage

This type of marriage, again, represents the fallen and ever lowered level of morals and upbringing of ignorant society. Those men sharing the pleasure of a woman have a perception that woman is a merchandise that can be bought and sold; that is, the woman can be exchanged between any two interested parties (similar to sharing an apartment or house). This sort of marriage is the main contributor to society's degradation, uncontrollable self indulgence and extreme focus on sensuality.

In the Hawaiian islands, until recently[17], several brothers were husbands to each others wives; the wives would accordingly belonged to each one of the brothers. Among the *Todas* tribe of India, the woman was also considered a wife to all younger brothers of her husband. In the same way each brother upon reaching adulthood would be her husband; also, each of the young sisters of the wife became the wife of all the brothers upon reaching adulthood. The children resulting from this mix would be distributed among the brothers according to their age and their seniority[18].

17. Collective (mixed) marriage

As mentioned before it is legally incorrect to call an improper and repellent sexual intercourse an act of marriage, but for the purpose of listing all marriages, including the gathering of men and women, this particular type should also be mentioned.

Collective marriage was practiced among the primitive tribes and still is in some parts of the world, in lieu of marriage. During the primitive times, the association of men and women was based on the natural sexual need without observance of any modesty or shyness or sense of expectation for any belonging or loyalty. This, of course, is very similar to animal gathering in collective manner. Later, in light of various influencing factors, association gradually took on a more orderly manner and finally evolved to the present form of marriage.

Historically, the old Indian tribe *Sountals* were pushed out of their natural habitat by Aryans and moved to the Himalayans, fully insulated from Buddhism or Hinduism. Until recently, they still maintained their original customs and perhaps even today all the young boys and girls gather once a year to marry one another. For six days and nights there is a total sex orgy among all. Later, every man and woman who had a liking for each other will dedicate themselves to that mate[19].

In Mexico of the 11th century, strict segregation of man and woman was enforced due to the treatment of women as inferior beings in that era. All women were forced to live, eat and sleep separately from men. Despite that, a group named *Ixuinames* existed whose people lived in absolute form of collective marriage; man and woman drank together and became intoxicated, performing all kinds of sensual activities. Such deviant behaviors, which sometime conveyed religious undertones by praising[20] human sacrifices took place under the supervision of their gods.

Morenhout in his travel journey to the Pacific region[21] on the subject of Tahiti and Marquises islands describes the habits of *Areois* group whose members had given their indulgences a religious flavor. They practiced their faith under the watchful observation of their god *Oro* the son of *Taaroa,* the great god of all Polynesians. Acceptance in such association was not easy. The applicant, first, had to work sometimes as a volunteer demonstrating his commitment and sincerity to the cause. Later on he would be given an opportunity to introduce himself to other members where a series of incantation and oral communication would be recited. At the end of the session, the applicant would express such an emotional sense of belonging that the group was convinced of his value as an additional member of the group.

The second stage of ritual in the presence of all members, involved a special swearing ceremonies performed in which any child presented as an "offering" would be killed. From that moment on a new member was officially acknowledged and as a new member of this sacred society, he could begin learning the special dances and songs of the group. Advancement to higher stages of the group would require additional sacrifices and expressions of more commitments. The significance of membership rank was designated by the number and type of the tattoos seen on their bodies.

The ultimate goal of this group was an absolute freedom of indulgence and sensuality with unconditional sexual relationship among men and women with no feelings of shame or modesty. Sacrificing of children was the condition for membership initiation as a duty for a man and woman. All women were common to all men and no couple's association lasted more than two to three days. Every mother was obligated to suffocate her newborn immediately after giving birth. If the newborn, for some reason, stayed alive for one half an hour his or her life was spared. A woman whose child had survived had to select a godfather among the crowd, at which time both parents would be ejected from the group; such rejects were then part of "the people with children".

Membership in this group was considered a privilege and prestige for men. The English explorer *Cook* took a Tahitian along to Great Britain. There, the Tahitian man claimed he considered his virtue and prestige not less than that of the King because he belonged to *Areois* group.

18. Loaned and exchanged marriage
This arrangement also demonstrated indulgence, sensuality and slavery to lust; it was another remnant of primitive collectiveness. Loaning and exchanging woman not only had been common in the past, but it is even practiced now. For example, members of the *Black Foot* tribe of the western part of North America, whose did in fact exchanged or loaned their wives with their friends.

In Greenland men loan their wives to their friends for a few months. This gesture is considered the greatest generosity, an ethical disposition, demonstrating extreme kindness and sincerity of the lender. The borrower, however, must return the temporary wife to her husband at an agreed date. Tribesmen of Africa and the Pacific Islands would rent their wives to white people and strangers routinely. In ancient Greece, this practice also had traces and as noted before, Socrates loaned *Gaziantep*'s wife to his friend *Alcibiades*. The mother of *Demos ten* the famous Greek orator was also subjected to the same treatment. In ancient Rome, Cato himself loaned his wife *Mercia* to his friend *Hortensius,* who subsequently returned to her husband after his friend's death[22].

19. Artificial versus real marriage

In this type of marriage, the husband contents himself with the name and title alone and there is no genuine attachment or interest in this relationship. In the Hawaiian Islands children are obligated to work for, and assist, their fathers. Some "fathers" were, however, only nominal husbands of their mothers. Under this scenario, the wife chooses her husband at her own volition, whereupon the children of her real marriage would officially, and for her convenience, belong to the nominal husband.

The *Reddies* clans arranged the marriage of a five year old boy with a twenty year old woman where the real husband is the uncle of the boy, but the children of this "marriage" would belong to the artificial father; that is, the *little* boy. He, in turn, after becoming an adult would marry a child(resulted from his previously arranged marriage when he was a child) to a twenty years old wife as it was done to him. Accordingly he will now possess the new "wife" for himself, and so on.

In *Mir*, Russia the father of a family, in recent years, acted as a suitor for his young boy and asked for their young daughter's hand. He then became her guardian until the young boy reached the age of puberty.

In Marco Polo's time, 13th century, the people of Mongolia would marry their dead children from one family to another in such a way that after conducting the necessary ceremonies for their marriage, including a marriage contract, they subsequently burn the documents, blowing the ashes into the wind dedicated to children's souls. This would indicate that the marriage had been fully consummated in this world. The result of this arrangement was that after the children of the two families were married to each other the two families would become relatives.

20. Three-quarter marriage
Among the people of African tribes, especially the Saharan, marriage was so arranged that the wife was free to do whatever she pleased one fourth of her married life; then she would exclusively belong to her husband for the other three quarters. Generally, the reference period was based on the division of days, that is, every four days. On the fourth day she would be free to live with anyone she chose with the provision that a child born in this manner would belong to the original couple.

21. Daily marriage
In some Pacific islands, the marriage relationship between a pair is specific to daytime and at night they do not recognized each other as such. In Australia and Tasmania the couple would only sleep together during the daytime because the inferiority of woman would not have permitted her to stay with her husband at night; additionally, the wife was supposed to have gone to other tribes entertaining their guests, particularly strangers.

22. Virginity marriage
For some African tribes, especially those influenced by Islam religion, woman's virginity is a pre-requisite for official marriage. The basic viewing of the necessity of this condition is the observance of chastity and piety since except by keeping their virginity, abstinence and maintenance of chastity of unmarried young woman can not be proven.

The morning of the day after the marriage consummation, the women on the side of bridegroom gather in the bedroom of the couple and accompanied by bride's relatives carefully investigate any signs of fresh blood. For the people of this tribe, disproving any claim of chastity is a cause for cancellation of marriage contract or the right of husband to do so. The laws of Islam do not prescribe the right of cancellation of marriage because there may be reasons other than lack of chastity (such as physical sport activities). The man, however, has the right to reduce the wife's dowry to a reasonable level that is practiced in cases of deflowered (non virgin) woman[23].

The young girls of *Rotouma* island who have kept their virginity the morning after the consummation, demonstrate their chastity and piety by painting their faces with red and green colors; they walk along public areas wearing their ornaments. Among the Jews, if the husband accuses his wife of having been deflowered she is condemned to be stoned unless her parents could prove to the elders that the accusation has been groundless. Among some African tribes the necessity of virginity gradually led to the exclusion of a widowed woman from marriage for a considerable period.

23. Deflowered (bride) Marriage
Contrary to the previous type of marriage, in some parts of the world the woman must be deflowered before her marriage. Here are some examples of this type of marriage practices.

In Sahara, Africa as noted the type of "purchased marriage" necessitates that the young women make their living by working as prostitutes.

In the Pacific Islands and among the indigenous tribes in India, young women are required to have been deflowered, by prostituting in the house of worship, prior to their marriage. In *Goa* and *Pondichery,* they would attend *Juggernaut* temple. Among the *Sakkalave* group, usually the mother and in case of procrastination, the girl herself would perform the deflowering act.

In Cambodia a special custom known as *Tchin-Than* had been practiced until about the 1880's. In every town once a year, on a specific day all young girls who have reached the right age would gather in a designated area. The religious leader of Buddha would agree to "purchase" all the girls for free. After the special ceremonies he would lead them to his quarters and upon performing intercourse with each one of them, he would later "resell" them to their respective parents for which he would collect handsome gifts. Afterwards, the girls would be allowed to get married[24].

In Malabar, India, when the chiefs and wealthy individuals marry their women, an "initiation" procedure requires that the virgin bride spend the first three nights with the grand religious leader, who upon delivering the deflowered bride to her husband, would collect his award of fifty gold coins.

24. Possessive Marriage

For the native American's the ownership and purchasing of a single wife was insufficient since he always had to be on his guard in order to protect his "property" from intruders. If a physically stronger man decided to possess his wife the weaker man would have to yield. Generally, those men who lacked the necessary skills for shooting (with bow and arrow) were, in practice, unable to, or prevented from, owning an attractive woman. This contention, as observed before, had its roots in animals where the female subject is offered to the strongest male animal. Among the Arabs (during the Period of Ignorance), a similar intrusion of privacy, i.e., attempts made to capture the wife of the weaker man which was sometime resisted by some defensive action. The well known *affaire d'honneur* (duels) practiced in the middle ages and until recently (19th century) in western countries was often caused by chasing women and a continuation of the primitive customs and habits. In ancient Rome, too, possessive marriage, as noted in chapter three of Part I, was one of the choices.

25. Multi-divorced (woman) marriage

Among some African tribes divorce is quite acceptable and common, so much so that the value and importance of a woman is dependent on the number of husbands she has had; as if divorce is embedded into the soul of marriage and that the woman must, within a few weeks, divorce her husband and remarry another man.

Not surprisingly, the widows remarry quicker as the frequency of their divorces increase. In the Sahara, a woman who has not changed husband is considered unimportant by other women since they believe she has not been an object of desire to more than one man.

In *Madagascar*, the waiting period (*Eddeh),* before remarrying is twelve days.

In *Ethiopia*, divorce is so prevalent that according to a world traveler a woman was observed to be sitting next to seven of her ex-husbands.

26. Converting old to new marriage

Some ignorant groups, particularly primitive Arabs, remarry simply by replacing a "used" wife to a new one. This act was routine and normal without any regard for the old, and even the loyal, wife. A woman who was divorced in this fashion, generally, would have less success when trying to remarry; her death and her divorce meant the same thing to her.

In contrast to the type of multi-divorced marriage, divorce was generally viewed as total disrespect and loss of prestige for woman among such tribes. This type of marriage usually applied to the wives who appeared to their husbands incapable of performing their duties or simply useless; otherwise those who had characters and were in charge of their family would be able to maintain their status.

One of the reasons for creating the rule of *loveira* (compulsory marriage of wife with deceased brother) was the belief that the widowed woman should be cared for and allowed to continue to belong to the family of deceased husband.

Prior to Islam, Arabs frequently divorced their wives and remarried with no apparent cause. Some started the process by defaming the wife, making her life so miserable that she gave up her dowry and wealth just to escape such wretchedness and disgrace. Her husband by extracting her wealth was then able to marry another woman. Islam denied this encroachment and injustice, prohibiting defamation of an innocent woman and any attempt to coerce her to give up her dowry and wealth[25].

27. Sheghar (the vacated) marriage

This type of marriage also belonged to Arabs of Period of Ignorance. It was a method of "vacating" in such manner that a man (as one side) would allow his daughter or sister to marry another man (as the other side) provided the other side would agree to do the same. The characteristic of this marriage had two advantages. First, the marriage required no dowry and second, the monetary benefit of "no-dowry" was transferred to the husband (father or brother in each side) instead of the rightful owner. Tn short the women to whom the men were being married would receive nothing from their husbands. Additionally, this marriage lacked the necessary conditions of the consent and permission of the subjected women. In reality, this type of marriage was another derivative of exchange marriage which, in turn, created and caused encroachment and injustice as observed in other marriages. It further stripped women of their rightful worth and character. The Prophet of Islam, by bestowing women their character and independence, cancelled and prohibited such practice; it is now an unacceptable method of marriage in most parts of the world.

General status of woman before Islam

The above listing and description of various types of marriage along with exotic and unfamiliar customs and habits of groups exhibit the extent to which women were exploited and considered inferior and worthless in the past is supported by the contents of previous chapters. The ignorance of humankind, regarding the status of women was so extensive that in Buddha's book of law, this delicate and trainable being was introduced as a wicked person in whom a special "sense" is placed for corrupting a man. It warned men to avoid being left alone with their sisters, mother or their own daughters. According to the Brahman book of law wife and daughter must obey their man as a shadow, whether dead or alive. Among the Indians, a widower must immediately re-marry, but if a widowed woman re-marries public sentiments would be dismayed.

In ancient China, during the engagement period should the bridegroom die, to preserve chastity and honor, it would be appropriate for the bride not to ever marry again. A chaste woman would preferably commit suicide upon the death of her spouse. A better way, yet, would be to commit suicide in a public square viewed by the crowd. Her name would then be engraved as a heroine.

In India woman must burn herself along with that of her dead husband. This habit was initially common among Bengals' higher echelon and later was propagated to the public; it had been cancelled only about fifty years ago (1880's). In the Indian state of *Mahabharata* two of the leaders, when they died, had seventeen wives and the other thirteen respectively. Twenty-one of these poor women surrendered themselves to fire. Another one who was pregnant did so after giving birth to her child.

Among the Celts, when a man wanted to know if his son was biologically his own, he would place him inside a basket and put the basket in a water stream. If the basket remained steady in the water the mother was safe and the child was legitimate, but if the basket had overturned, the child was drowned and the mother would be killed.

In Assyria *Hammurabi* laws saved women from their tragic past. Nevertheless if the woman was not mindful of home economic, causing her husband "damages to their home" or left the house, returning to her family without her husband's permission or caused any disturbances, the man had a right to discharge her without any dowry or keep her as a servant while taking another wife. The husband could also drown her if proven to the court of law that she had committed any material waste or self-indulgence. In the event the judge's ruling favored the wife, she would only be entitled to her dowry as a divorcee. If, however, the husband was proved to be right the court's ruling would be drowning. Prior to *Hammurabi* laws the woman had no rights whatsoever to plea for her case. If a woman ever declined her husband's wishes she would be immediately drowned.

The coming of Moses and his Book of Law was not sufficient or able to save Israeli women from misery and disgrace. Among the Jews, like the Arabs of Period of Ignorance, the birth of a female child was shameful and considered a dishonor. The mother who had given birth to a girl was declared unclean for fifteen days. She had to wash herself for another seventy days consecutively. This timeframe would be reduced to thirty five days if the child was male. On the day of the male child's birth twenty units of the current money was given as alms; this compared to ten units for a female child. Woman was completely obedient to her husband. Permission for marriage (of woman) rested with the guardian of the woman; while divorce was originated from the husband's wish and desire. The female children were sold and prayer of a woman was counted as half of the man. In the Torah, it is said: "when a man purchased a Jewess from her father and after she has served for six years she should be freed on the seventh year".

Christianity improved woman's situation in Europe, although Jesus made no distinction between man and woman in his conversations and he would address women as he addressed men, but he preferred to live as single man rather than marry. Marriage remained as unpleasant as before until the coming of Islam. Marriage, based on Islam's teachings and as detailed in the next chapter, ultimately ended all the injustices and transgressions imposed on women and improved their social status and prestige in all possible ways.

CHAPTER TWO
Marriage according to Islam
and European jurisprudence

A) Marriage according to Islam

Islam's Sharia treats this serious *social* contract with utmost importance and institutes its foundations on conventions and intellect as well as moral fundamentals.

Islam, in contrast to Christianity (catholicism) which has promoted celibacy(abstaining from marriage and sexual relations), has offered significant encouragement and moral support to its followers regarding marriage. No other social affair is more recommended or promoted as marriage and its linkage to reproduction and the continuity of mankind by means of forming a family. The Prophet of Islam has constantly encouraged people to marry.

"The unluckiest of you are those who are not married and die as bachelor".

Anyone who avoids an unalterable natural custom and common morality, will remain deficient and as such will be unlucky because the ultimate goal is to achieve happiness in life. The Prophet's encouragement and praising of giving birth and continuity of self is further expressed as:

"The real reason for the absence of marriage, is reproduction)" and, *"to many of you, even the miscarried, o' Muslims, I will honorably take pride over other people, on the Day of Reckoning".*

Islam has not made any provision as pre-conditions that may cause delay in the execution of a marriage contract. This is in contrast to divorce which can be suspended due to its many obligations and conditions and troubles, resulting in delay and sometime, postponement that could essentially make the case irrelevant, if and when the causes are removed. There is no exigency condition stipulated in marriage other than protecting the rights of the parties as it is incorporated in all marriage contracts. Even the poor and underprivileged[1] have been promised that if married the grace of God would make them enabled and independent.

This glad tiding and hope originate from Islam's perception of marriage as unification and splicing whose focused purpose is cooperation of two human beings, equal in every respect and as companions. They would assist each other in easing any difficulties in their lives and while enjoying legitimate pleasures of life they nurture their children, with mutual assistance, preparing them to join the society. Both parents devote their efforts, in a conducive environment and with complete sincerity, to establish a home filled with pure love and quality life, free from any doubt and hard feelings and cleansed of two-faced and double-dealing characters.

It is clear that the result of this partnership and cooperation would be nothing but the goodness and blessing comfort. Additionally, the mere act of being married and responsible for family subsistence will awaken

136

and intensify, many times, the faculty of human activities, that would otherwise be inactive and abated during the bachelorhood.

It is often observed that the whimsical and arbitrary young people who make the least amount of effort in creating and managing their wealth, will quickly change direction in both fronts after they are married. The responsibility of managing their family affairs will make them wiser in spending, and more prudent in conserving.

In order to institute the social fabric of Muslim societies and establish their families on a sound and strong foundation, Islam first prohibited, and fought strongly against, indecency and mixed illegitimate marriage which were considered the source of corrupting the instinctive repro-duction. Islam, then promoted marriage and encouraged Muslims with varied means on various grounds. To achieve this noble cause, Islam had to transform life style from its indecent and shameful form into a model to fit the ideal society whose people, in turn, would possess a clear mind.

1. Definition, terms and properties

Islam, promoted marriage and encouraged Muslims with varied means and various grounds for optimism. To achieve this noble cause, Islam transformed the life style from its indecent and shameful form into a model to fit the ideal society whose people, in turn, regained a clear mind. That is why Islam, in this endeavor, attended to several key topics.

a) Definition

As previously mentioned, Islam has placed a signboard of affection and love as preface to the book of marriage, positioning the parties of this important social contract as owners of two gentle and kind hearts and minds. Islam announced equal creation of man and woman from a sin-gle grain; acknowledging the physical formation of Eve as that part of Adam's sidelong, and joining these two equal and similar beings attested to complete sincerity and purity[2].

Since man and woman are created from the same gem neither has an advantage over another. God created woman as part of the side of man not from his upper part to allow woman to dominate man, nor from the lower side to allow man to humiliate woman. God created a woman from the long-side of a man for her to be an equal ally and a companion to a man. She is near his heart and intimately close to his inner soul, that is, a source for producing love of togetherness, kindness and mercy between the two of them.

None of the religious or civil laws, of the past or most recent, provided such definition of marriage. Today that social science has been elevated in most cultures and anthropologists have been successful in discovering its secrets, one can appreciate the import of this ethical and social definition presented thirteen hundred years ago in the midst of the unlettered and primitive part of the world.

Today's civilization has made information available to mankind, beyond any comparison to fourteen hundred years ago. Man is now aware of thousands secrets of nature and can influence and control world's materials and beyond by exploring nature's elementary particles. Man has come to understand that the stem of continuity of the universe is love and friendship. Man understands that unlimited and infinite forces of attraction that exist in every being, secure its continuity. The gravity of sun keeps the earth in suspension in space; other stars gravitate, in relative terms, towards each other. This attraction force can be noted in every aspect of life arena, with different circumstance and varied performance.

Among parents and children and relatives, this gravity leads to affection; between man and woman gravity leads to love; between friends and partners gravity leads to friendship and truthfulness; between any two physical matters gravity leads to chemical balance and coexistence in harmony; and between two solid matters there is gravitational force. The circumstances upon which this force would influence the principles and is manifestation of life, is beyond human understanding. The absence of the alchemy of universal force of attraction will cause disintegration of human societies as well as those of biological, botanic, solid matters and heavenly elements.

Human love may be classified as follows:

1. Sexual reproductive love between male and female

2. Blood-related love:

   a) among parents, children, brothers and other near relations;

   b) friendship and affection among friends and acquaintance;

   c) patriotism among people of a nation and love for their nationality.

3. Intelligent love which is the love of mankind to anything beautiful and useful

The genesis and mother of all kinds of love is selfishness and love of self, which in itself, should be considered the sole drive for continuity of the existence. The first group, the sexual love, is of prime interest.

Sexual love as an instinct is endowed in any living creature especially, the advanced class of beings. The existence of this instinct causes the continuity and expansion of the kind and its absence leads to extinction of mankind. The growth and intensity of this instinct would be a function of natural selection.

The above tradition was based on the principle of struggle for existence which engages all creatures in a universal battleground. The instinctive love caused the creation and the continuity of this endeavor; it persisted as long as life went on. The outcome was the survival of more competent and more accomplished while the defective and incomplete ones waned. To implement the custom of continuing better creatures another principle is needed, that being the natural selection. The nature selected the strong and capable for lasting-ness, enabling one with the tools necessary for its defense in order to maintain continuity. The necessary tools for continuity included fortifying reproduction, instinct and sexual desire. As a result the strengthening of reproducing instinct, was based on natural selection choices. For the societies which were not fit for continuity this instinct was in the form of excessiveness and greed or atrophy and abatement. As a noble cause, the prophets and social reformers attempted to moderate this natural instinct in order to ensure the continuity of life.

At any event, sexual love is strongest and most active than other body's lively constituents. This phenomenon is considered "lust" among animals and "love" among mankind. The difference between these two interpretations is that lust is a reproducing instinct and applies to animals satisfying their natural need of male and female upon availability and attraction. That is not so between man and woman. Love between a man and woman has the characteristic of man loving one woman only and cannot satisfy his need with any other woman except connecting with her. Therefore, lust is a general sexual instinct while love represents feelings, both selective and preferred.

In the beginning, the requirement for continuity of nature's wide-spread variety of creatures, caused the advent of love among humankind as well as animals; so the source and the flagship of love was the reproductive archetype. Yet, the approach of male towards the female, whether animal or man, was not the intent of the instinct of reproducing. The inclination was only for satisfying one's lust and pleasure as well as relief from pain. Some men even prevented the act of reproducing. That is why nature focusing on reproduction, has innovated this natural instinct in human and animal, added with physical pleasure, above all other acts, to ultimately ensure that reproducing was accomplished. After the human attraction elevated to the stage of love, it was love that caused the reproduction because the attraction in the first stage was based on feelings, originating from the soul as well as the love of beauty. In the next stage, this inclination led to uniting of man and woman by employing the tools for reproduction.

Love has three elements; two distinct beings and a force, as third element, causing the two "distinct beings" as elements coming together. The two elements are man and woman; the third element, is affection and friendship. One can liken love to water which is formed by Oxygen and Hydrogen as two elements and the force of chemical friendship as the third element. The essence of love consists of the following components.

b) Reproduction instinct
This inherent aptitude is the strongest type of love that exists in all intelligent animals including humankind; it is more or less non-existent in the rest of animals. This instinct is no less than hunger with respect to the "force it exerts" and its "effect on the subject", except that the former ensures the coming into "being of the type" in the future, while the latter is the guarantor of the life of the type at present. When the season is right, the climate condition is favorable and there is no obstacle then, there is naturally an inclination within all living creatures, male or female; hence attraction.

c) Admiring beauty
As mentioned before, sexual love is interpreted as love for humankind and as lust for animal; the difference being that humankind falls in love with a recognizable proper form of body and beauty; therefore one is open to the usage of natural selection. Sexual love after it is *purified* and has reached the level of love is called spirited love and in the same manner that love distinguishes human from animal in terms of sexual desire, the scale of civility and maturity of human sentiments and feelings would also represent the high and low levels of this kind of love,

both quantitatively and qualitatively. Love among primitive tribes often did not extend beyond reproducing instinct. On the contrary, civilized societies go beyond reproducing instinct, by paying attention to beauty of the person independently. The impression that beauty, combined with spiritual love, makes on a civilized man is so strong, that at times, it eclipses the reproducing instinct, acquiring its own independence and personality.

Of course the maturity of human sentiments is the result of evolution of civil societies and its growth is limited to that of nation's civilization and its openness because its literary, ethical and social outcome for men have a direct impact on their sensitivity.

Obviously, a woman who is the object of love and affection due to her beauty and proper form of body will not ever be living in captivity as a weak and despicable being; neither will she be deprived from her civil and social rights. Men who recognize elegance in a woman can- not show disrespect for her. On the other hand, since love for beauty, reinforces the traditional way of selection (of mate). Men generally seek women who are good looking, chaste, efficient who does not betray their love. Women look for men who can protect them through strength, who are noble and will behave as gentlemen; men who do not commit any injustice and hardship, respecting their rights. Women also look for those men who are zealous in standing firm and protect their latitude.

It can then be said the love of beauty and the "way" of selection have been instrumental in humankind's ethical excellence and, in turn, this grace and noble temperament will elevate the level of civility within the societies. It is equally true, that man's thought process has been appreci- ably refined due to historical evolution in different civilizations, as well as other causes. It is this refinement which has been instrumental in transforming the sexual instinct to the realm of love and appreciation of beauty. The conclusion is then drawn that the quality of love among the members of a society is proportional to the ethical and social position-ing (of individuals) with mutual effect.

What is beauty?

Beauty is gentleness and softness as well as suitability governed between the observer and the observed. The observed can be a person or an object of interest. The source of this gentleness and suitability always resides with the observer. It is because of this appeal that a specific face appears beautiful in someone's view, while others may observe no such beauty at all. The following masterpiece of Persian poetry describes the concept of beauty.

"If you are (in place of) Majnnon you will not see beauty, butt in Leily.

Caliph said to Leily:
Is it you who made Majnoon so confused and lost?
You are no better than other beauties.
Be quiet, she said, you are no Majnoon."

Such illusion is caused by continuous sensation of nervous system; additionally, the association through affection and the habit of recogniz-ing beauty were major contributors. The first time that a man felt affec-tion and love within himself, a form and figure appeared beautiful to him, from a particular point of view, perceived as a basis and measure of beauty. Later, according to familiarity and force of habit, no distinction could be made between ugly and beautiful. A man does not enjoy music of foreign land because of lack of familiarity and a habit of not listening to that music. The primitives and some African tribes, by wearing orna-ments, enjoy looking at large wooden or metallic ring embedded in their nose or lips. As such, everyone for the love of beauty longs for a "perfect prototype of beauty" perceived in one's mind. To form this perception, man noted particular characteristics of beauty by observing each of the faces in his surroundings, whether physical or beyond that. By drawing a picture of some combinations of these characteristics, man developed a perfect prototype of beauty in his mind, always searching for one such beauty in the real world.

At last, assisted by fusion of perceptions and association of ideas, human is allowed to look for one or two virtues and visual image of beauty and assume that such combination of properties or characteristics, residing in one individual shall suffice to encompass all the other specific properties that he had looked for. A proverb expresses this sentiment.

"All things good people possess are in you alone."

Of course, an analytic mind blocks out all these claims laid out, but the over-powering sexual love and the reproduction instinct strongly support the assertions made in favor of logical reasoning:

"He (Majnoon) was able to focus through his intelligence;
but his envisioning of Leily robbed him of that."

d) Inclining and imploring
The feelings for affection are also considered as one component of love. The animals express this as their love reserved for the time of marrying, during the monthly period and when nurturing the child; whereas for humankind love and feelings are expressed at all times. Inclination and appealing for love, attract lover to the beloved.

The lover is happy when the beloved has the good fortune and saddens when the beloved is in discomfort. Man tries hard to amass wealth and acquire fame to please the beloved. He is inclined to possess the attributes that would please the beloved while making sincere effort to relieve the beloved from pain and hardship.

e) Just virtue
The biggest agent of mental love is the goodness of virtue; its absence removes any distinctions between humankind love and a four-legged

animal. Virtue is implanted on the first day of nurturing in the atmosphere of love. The commencement of practicing righteous virtue, such as truth, justice, mercy, courtesy and perceptiveness, begins on the day that the inclination towards such virtues is felt by human. The first virtue that manifests itself is the just virtue with respect to man's beloved. Practice of just virtue, would make it a habit of just virtue; it spreads among relations, friends, colleagues and fellow citizens. The lover tries to assure the beloved that he is self-inclusive of all traits of virtue.

The dishonorable and the inferiors find lesser meaning of love in a true sense. They are often caught in carnal desire of a four legged animal. If they express love to, or marry someone most of them will possess a supposed refined and cultivated virtue. Their virtue is crude and discourteous.

In short, love is the educator of virtue and manifestation of humankind.

f) Sacrifice

Forfeiture is also an expression of and the causality for spiritual love. In a four legged-animal act of lust there is no sign of this sacrifice and personal loss. If there appears to be any such thing its analytic interpretation can be traced to selfishness and self adoration; whereas, in a "spiritual love", love, and sacrifice have many manifestations.

On certain occasions, sacrifice goes beyond the love of personage. Lover for the pleasure of beloved, foregoes his own pleasure and interest, even to the cost of sacrificing. Mother is willing to surrender her life to save her child from a danger. Woman is willing to sell her belongings and spend it on her husband to save him from hardship. Staying up until dawn, caring for sick spouse at his (her) bedside. One can therefore state that love generates just virtues and sacrifice is its outstanding manifestations as well as an ethical generosity

g) Respect

Since the lover observes all appearances of goodness, dignity and honor as well as beauty in the beloved he considers her greater in importance and more honorable in nobility than himself. It follows that man and wife feel an eternal mutual affection towards each other as they constantly respect each other. Respect is one of the required signs of friendship.

Based on the above-mentioned topics, the importance of love, this strong arm of universal order, becomes evident as well as its effect on, particularly, humankind's societies. Basically, the reason for stating that humankind, in contrast to animals, is created naturally to socialize within a civil society is that no individual can live without the assistance and support of another in order to satisfy all his needs. As such, affection and kindness found among humans would outstrip that of animals. A human child before reaching adolescence will be in need of affection and assistance of parents and this period of childhood is quite long. In contrast the child of animal of tender year after a very short period will be free from parental needs, living independently.

This difference is observed in a long period that parents spend in nursing and nurturing their child. The short period of animal childhood, necessary for animal's parents, should not be interpreted as lesser opportunity for expressing affection towards the animal child; in contrast to the lengthy period for human child's, as well as the intensity of affectionate feelings expressed by the human child's parents. No, that is not so. The apparent shortening of the period for animals parental affection, has made the nature to equip the animal child with necessary means for the protection and survival in a very short time, enabling them to live independently. For human the existence of intense affection of parents, with lengthening of childhood period, necessitates the quality of child's need for assistance and for this reason humankind embraces socialization in a natural way with growing sense of mutual assistance and cooperation. In the same manner, mutual affection between man and wife brings about cooperation in their social life.

There is no doubt that creation of a family and its continuity is dependent on the affection of man and wife to each other and their tenderness towards their children; the families, in turn, form the foundation of societies. The animals do not approach one another, except for satisfying their need for lust and immediately after relief they separate from each other. The children after a few days must also meet their own needs and earn their living. Accordingly, social gathering among animals is meaningless, while humans regardless of lust, approach each other on the basis of fondness and affection, and take care of their children. Hence, the source of society's strength is love.

World's religions and theological virtues will only grow and stand firm against events and changes in time- if their laws are compiled and organized in accordance with the unalterable tradition or the laws of nature. Sharia, the laws of Islam, is the most comprehensive religious teachings that in each one of its rules and directives cite the principles and unchangeable fundamentals of creation, harmonizing its laws with those of nature's customs, traditions and creation.

Religion of Islam, has founded the civic society based on family formation whose essence is affection and compassion. There is a European proverb that shows how much tenderness and affection between man and wife would be worth:

"Woe to a woman who learns affection from other than her husband. A woman who marries a man for whom she has no love has (already) travelled half a distance to depravation".

It is worth noting the definition that Islam offers for marriage. It is inclusive of all secrets and issues which science, technology and knowledge, in general, have discovered in today's civilized humankind. The necessary existence of feelings and affectionate relationship between man and wife confirm the freedom of their choice. How could it be possible for a man to have any affections for a woman whom he has not seen or known? On the contrary, the interpretation of the Qur'an verse[3] shows the absolute freedom of choice between the two of them for marriage contract. As it will be seen later, no marriage in Sharia Law is considered appropriate and legitimate unless the parties to the contract are made aware of all physical and intellectual particulars of each other that would bear upon their identity.

2) Rights of man and wife
Despite the past and then current tribal rules and habits, Islam first took upon reforming the rights of the parties to marriage. Islam glorified woman by granting her attribute and independence in her resoluteness. The women of 7th century enjoyed the privileges of choice and freedom which were denied to the European women until 16th century. A young Muslim woman had the right to marry any man whom she chose even against her parents wishes. She was only required to inform her guardian. In the event the guardian did not consent without offering any acceptable objection to the marriage, the Magistrate (of community or town) would proceed with concluding the marriage contract. A marriage contract of an under-age girl signed by her guardian was only proper and valid if the girl, after reaching puberty, had given her consent. When one of Prophet's assistants[4] had married her daughter to a man without her consent, he ruled the marriage as void and the girl on her own volition married someone else[5]. The Second Caliph[6], censured a man who attempted to hide his old age from her young wife-to-be by coloring his beard because of deception.

After the marriage contract is sealed, Islam has given the husband the right to expect accommodation, sincerity and loyalty from his wife; the woman is equally has the right to expect affection, common benefit and undertaking of sustenance from her husband.

On nurturing and teaching, the right and duty of man and wife is based on equality in a manner that not only the woman is entitled to spend some of her time for education, even without the consent of her husband, but she may demand education from her husband by any required means. The Prophet is quoted to have said: "It is the wife's duty to obey her husband and express her sincerity to him; not permitting anyone to their home without the consent of her husband and it is incumbent upon the husband to express his appreciation to his wife and not raising his voice". It is notable that although in all matters of life obeying of husband and acquiring his consent is necessary, when the matter of learning and education becomes the issue the wife does no longer require her husband's consent and she is allowed to proceed even over his objection.

In short, Islam established the rights of the parties, man and wife, on the basis of equality[7]. In the event of dispute between the parents, the right of educating of child is given to the father, but at the same time the right of nurturing at early age (boys for two years and girls for 7 years) is given to the mother because father has a larger share in development of child[8] as far as law of nature is concerned.

The rationale is that the father is in stronger position than the mother to undertake the training of the child in physical fitness and capability and the intellectual as well as cognitive development. On the other hand, during the first few years, the new born child will need the attention and caressing of mother more than ever and the security of being with the father is not sufficient by itself to compensate for satisfying child's natural needs.

Islam considers the management of the family and decision making, on all matters of living conditions, as well as maintaining the external family relationships as specialties of man, while the organization and conducting the internal matters of household are the rights and specialties of woman. Islam has established woman in her family home as a powerful self-willed person. The right of divorce is given to husband against the money received by his wife as performance bond. At the same time, the woman has the right that under certain circumstances when reason and fairness justify, to ask for divorce or to cancel the marriage contract[9]. Further, Islam has recognized the right, as explained in detail later, of both man and woman conducting their financial affairs independently from one another.

3) Duties of man and wife

An important duty of man in marriage is that of providing income and being responsible for the sustenance of his family. Islam took into account that the physical nature of woman's feebleness, fragility and tenderness as compared to man's natural strength. Accordingly, Islam viewed woman with mercy and compassion, while not neglecting to extend reverence towards her. Islam mitigated the wife from payment of the necessary family expenses, which is the responsibility of man in return for his expectations from his wife. Islam was committed the man to hire a wet nurse if the wife is unable or unwilling to nurture the child herself. Additionally, man was required to pay the performance bond (*Mehrieh*) as part of marriage contract upon her demand. Duties of woman were obeying her husband, expressing her sincerity and loyalty to her husband and managing the internal affairs of the household, including childcare. Islam carefully detailed the division of labor in terms of each party's ability and specialty in terms of performing the specific and specialized tasks in the best fashion.

Today, this method of job allocation based on the field of specialization is extensively utilized as part of division of labor in the field of economics. Under ideal conditions, everyone is assigned to a job for which he is a natural candidate[10].

To require a woman to participate in sustenance necessitates that women also partner in social affairs and general work force and this undertaking will cause her to be hindered from her specialized task, namely, giving birth, nurturing children and managing the internal matters of home. Since woman is definitely not stronger than man and is not able to perform two different tasks; hence the reason behind woman being excused from participation in living expenses. Instead the responsibility for the family subsistence is only placed with the man. Daughters and wife must be supported by the husband, and in absence of the husband the son is charged with mother's livelihood.

The notable point is that a father must support a boy's livelihood who happens to be poor and weak until such time that he is capable of supporting himself. A father can force his son who is of age and healthy to make a living, but cannot do the same with his daughter unless she undertakes the task willingly and make her own living whereupon father is not required to support her. Supporting a daughter is father's obligation until she is married, at which time the husband will take over the responsibility of supporting her. If she is divorced except for the duration of waiting period her father is again responsible for supporting her. After the father and husband are deceased the subsistence of all women in the family is the responsibility of the son. In any case, Islam is mindful of woman's elegance of body and compassion of her soul and therefore has assigned the responsibility of this difficult and tiresome matter of sustenance a special attribute of man.

4) Financial affairs of parties
Islam allows women, both married and single, to conduct their own financial affairs, freely and independently. They include purchase and sale, property rental, settlement of dispute, partnership and all legal transactions related to her personal wealth. Although wife must obey her husband in all matters related to their living conditions, he has no right to express any legal or official opinion regarding her financial affairs under any circumstances. Not only whatever she owns is hers and on the choice of managing and spending she alone is the decider, but as mentioned in previous section there is no set of rules in place to obligate her to make any contribution to the living expenses and that is why her share of inheritance is one half of the man.

In practice, however, among most Muslim families, sincerity and perfect purity which exist between man and wife would cause the woman to surrender the control of her entire wealth to her husband and by giving him a full power of attorney as her legal representative she will obey his decisions. She would even let him make contributions from her income towards supplementing household expenses. This kind of trust and good behavior is the result of affection and complete understanding that should always exist between man and wife and accordingly would never require any legalization. While woman is free and independent in her financial affairs, she shares happiness and difficulties of life, wealth and poverty, joy and misery with her husband, blessed by sentiment and human feelings at its best. The sacred focal place, wherein there is tranquility and where any sign of husband's annoyance is cleared or removed, is the home of eastern families. These societies are structured around families that still enjoy such virtuous trait and for which the French philosopher *Gustave Laboune* longed. Its pure environment is filled with truth and pleasantness, in which every sad heart is turned into a happy and blissful one.

In conclusion, woman from the point of view of Islam is an elegant being who is fashioned as an equal creation to man, and an independent person. While her fineness and soul pleasing is notable, her mental strength and her equality with man are also recognized. This is in contrast to interpreting woman's mental elegance as weakness by other laws and beliefs. Had they discovered, in a civilized world, any strength in her she would have been employed to do hard labor, with her tender skin being subjected to the fire and heat of factory plants and foundries. Islam, on the one hand recognizes woman as an independent and competent person to select her own husband and be in charge of her own destiny as well as handling her own financial dealings. On the other hand, Islam is not ignoring her soul quality, tenderness of sentiment, feelings and her elegant body. Firstly, woman is free to do whatever she wishes with her wealth; secondly, she is exempt from any payments towards household and family expenses. As explained in the following section, the civilized world has wronged this tender kind of human being because neither of the two particular rights of woman are being observed in their societies.

B-Marriage: French Jurisprudence

General: Written in1804, French Civil Code states that man and woman as adolescents are free to choose. Although the legal age for both sexes is twenty-one years, for marriage, the ages of eighteen for man and fifteen for woman are acceptable, as per articles 144 and the subsequent ones. Outside of these age limits, and in special cases arising from moral and social interests, a waiver (for marrying a couple) must be issued by the President of the Republic. Prior to the age of twenty-one in addition to both parties' consent that of the parents are also required. In the event of disagreement between any two parents father's consent will be preferred[11]. In the event that parents are deceased the consents of grand parents are required and in their absence, a family council comprising relatives of both parents must document a written consent, but its submission to the public notary may be oral. From the age of twenty-one to twenty five instead of consent of parents, consulting the parents followed by their blessing in presence of public notary will be adequate. Previously this was needed until such time that both parties had reached the age of thirty. Additionally, the married couple were required to inform, by means of official declaration, their parents of their qualitative married conditions three times within the period of three months. The new changes have reduced the age of thirty to twenty five and the frequency of reporting the marriage status from three times to one time. Article147 specifies that the second marriage is not allowed unless the first one is annulled[12]. Article 160 prohibits incestuous marriage[13].

1. Legal proceeding:

There are two stages of legal proceeding. First, the pre-marriage protocols and the second, ceremonies that are concurrently required. The most important custom of the past is the public announcement containing the subject of marriage and the identity of the couple. This is done through the local municipality which posts the information on the notice board within its premises. This notice must be visible to public as seen by all for the period of ten days in order for everybody to know the content. The intent of the legislature for such notice is to let the official of

Notary Office be informed of any problem or legal impasse that may be perceived by the interested party regarding this matter. The official of Notary Office will stop the proceedings based on any objections made until such time that the objection is removed either by the order of the court or voluntary withdrawal of objector. The person raising objection is, most likely, previous wife of the presumed husband, who is not yet divorced. Her objection is based on illegality of his second marriage. It is also possible that parents of bride are not consenting to marrying of their under-age daughter.

In assessing the qualification of Notary, the residency of the couple must be taken into account. Marriage of foreigners in France, in order to be recognized in French court of law, must obey the same laws and procedures. Marriage of French citizen in foreign lands will be under the jurisdiction of the country of residence[14]. Upon returning to France, their marriage must be recorded in their identification card by the public Notary official. In case the couple are both French citizens they must report to their embassy in the country of residence for embassy official to record the notary public proceedings.

2. Duties of the couple

i) Subsistence: Article 213 states that living expenses is not an exclusive duty of husband; both man and wife can proportionally to their income be responsible for family subsistence. Later in this section, detail of the method of this arrangement is described.

ii) Loyalty: The couple must mutually express their sincerity and remain faithful to each other, but the laws make two distinctions between man and wife. One is penal(punishable by law), the other is civil. Adultery if committed by the wife always and, at any rate, is subject to legal prosecution following her husband's complaint. If man commits adultery, the wife can take her husband to court if he has had an affair with an estrange woman even if occurred only one time at the family residence. Legally, adultery if committed by woman under any conditions gives the man the right of divorce. However if man commits adultery except in the above-mentioned case, the woman is denied the right of divorce. This particular clause is now canceled, but the difference still remains in case of criminal prosecution.

iii) Residency: Article 214 bounds the woman to live in the residence chosen by her husband, but if he changes the residency more frequently than normal this duty of woman to follow her husband is voided.

iv) Protection and obedience: Article 213 succinctly comprises one of the duties and fundamental rights of the parties. Husband must protect his wife and the wife must obey her husband. This mutual right and duty of parties is considered one of the fundamental pillars of marriage in French jurisprudence. As such the legislature has established supremacy of man over woman and since the intent has been to maintain this superiority and its legal preference as the basis for family formation, the couple is not allowed to arrive at a mutual consent and to conclude a separate agreement between them. This preferential jurisdiction and (legal) authoritarian rule of the man has caused lack of competencies and therefore deficiency regarding any financial authorization for woman. In other words, women after marrying have systematically lost a series of rights and authorities, making them subservient and docile to their husbands wishes.

In the past several years the women's rights societies comprising learned people and scholars of law, both men and women, have attempted to overturn the privileges given to men and to grant the married women their due rights, but as yet (late 60's) no tangible results have been achieved[15].

Articles 215 and 217 describe the consequences of incompetencies of women. A married woman cannot execute any legal transaction by herself and without her husband's permission. Any transactions would need permission from her husband. In the event that husband denies her the permission without acceptable excuse she can file a complaint in the court of law. Upon proving the legitimacy of transaction she can obtain a court order to proceed. The husband's permission, in addition to affirmation of wife's action, would be a confirmation to the joint responsibility of man and wife in contrast to a court order which clears the husband from any responsibility[16].

Court's order or husband's permission is always limited to specific case as requested by the wife. The grantor must specify the case for which the permission is granted. The husband cannot award a blank permission for all transactions to his wife because in such circumstance the legislature's intent of wife's obeying her husband is breached. Nevertheless, if the wife wants to engage in trading it will suffice for the husband to generally agree for his wife to buy and sell goods. A general permission for daily purchases of food stuff and household goods, if she is given such responsibility, will be adequate.

The following three cases of exception are made for which the husband's permission is not needed.

i) Drawing up a will: The reason is that otherwise she would be influenced by him that may be against her interest and that of other beneficiaries. The rationale for this exception is that this will, would become effective upon the wife's death and accordingly the marriage contract is no longer valid. Her obeying of the husband is required only when the marriage is in place; therefore, independence of woman in this case is not contradicting the basic premiss of the legislature.

ii) In 1881, a law, regarding national savings account was enacted, which allowed married women to deposit and withdraw funds from that account as an independent saver. The rationale for this exception was apparently to encourage people to save.

iii) A woman who is physically separated from her husband and lives away from her husband is independent with regards to her legal transactions. In light of article 311, the reason for this exception would become clear[17].

Any transactions executed by married woman without her husband's permission, as in the case of minors or mentally unfit person, is subject to cancelation. Man and wife independently applying for cancelation can appear in the court as private plaintiff and so can their legal beneficiaries. The statutory limitation for cancelation request is ten years.

3. Cancelation of marriage contract

pre-amble- The principle of contract cancellation in French jurisprudence is either absolute or relative.

i) The absolute cancellation applies to a situation where the occurrence of the transaction will damage public order or good deeds of the society or country. In this type of absolute transaction the task of evaluating the instance and whether there are sufficient grounds for canceling the contract, or not will rest with the court of law. For absolute transaction cancellation public prosecutor, from public aspect of it, can in absence of plaintiff file a complaint requesting cancellation of contract. Since it is related to public affair cancellation cannot be confirmed by the parties involved.

ii) The relative cancellation of contract usually refers to personal interests of the parties that are threatened. For relative contract cancellation, the court cannot and does not make any evaluation of the private affair since the law itself has addressed specific instances. In a relative transaction cancellation the presence of plaintiff is definitely required and the claim cannot be prosecuted. Since the relative cancellation of contract is related to personal interests the transaction that is to be cancelled can be confirmed by the interested party. The relative cancellation of contract is monopolized by two issues. The lack of competency and the absence of consent. With regards to the absence of consent between the parties it may be due to coercion, mistake or deception.

The two types of cancellations also differ with respect to statute of limitation, where there is no mention of time and therefore it follows the standard thirty years for absolute cancellation, but for relative contract cancellation the period of ten years applies. This statutory period, however, in most cases, is extended because if the cause of cancellation is that a party being a minor, the start of statutory limitation is the beginning of adolescence and in case of married woman it is the cancellation of marriage; and if there is a lack of satisfaction of either party the start of statutory date is the date when dissatisfaction of a party is established. The attention should now be directed towards an important application of cancellation of marriage contract.

a) Regarding the case of absolute cancellation, although in principle and in general it is assessed by the court of law, with respect to marriage contract the law specifically has enumerated the issues that make the marriage contract absolutely null and void and as such the court has no authority to make any assessment. Under the following five cases the marriage contract is considered cancelled

i)   Man or wife has not (or both have not) reached the legal age of fifteen for woman and eighteen for man[18];

ii) Polygamy;

iii) Incestuous marriage;

iv) Secret marriage (without the involvement of notary public record);

v)   Disqualified officer of Notary public record.

b) The relative cancellation of marriage contract, also has gone through some changes.

To start, one of the three causes for lack of consent is eliminated; that being deception. If the marriage contract is challenged due the absence of consent which is based on deception the case is not considered by the court; because if deception becomes a cause for cancellation there will be few marriage contracts that have legal standing. A well known French jurist *Oisel* says, "On the subject of marriage, everyone who can, will deceive."

There are then two causes for absence of consent; erroneousness and coercion. There are three types of erroneousness. Physical, legal and moral. The physical erroneousness is when one of the married couple has been switched to another look-alike person, disguising his (her) age or face. The legal erroneousness is one of the married couple's identification documents belong to someone else. The moral erroneousness refers to particular temper and special characteristic of one of the married couple being missing, but French courts do not take notice of this last kind of error because of its frequent occurrence and in fact it is similar to deception.

Another topic which the legislature has erred from the basic principle relates to the period during which, filing of the complaint is possible. As explained before, the statute of limitation for relative cancellation of all transactions is ten years. On the other hand, articles 181 and 202 of French civil code states: "If a wife or husband is discontented with the marriage due to error or coercion and yet submits to cohabitation the statute of limitation for filing for cancellation is reduced to six months"; otherwise the statute of limitation remains as ten years.

A lack of qualification for marriage contract means the couple not having reached the age of adolescence[19,] namely, twenty-one years, while not securing their parents consent to their marriage. Or, if the couple are aged between twenty-one and twenty five years, but have not "consulted with their parents before the marriage. The complaint may be filed by one of the couple or anyone whose consent would have been required such as parents or associated family members. According to article 182, the public prosecutor or other relations of the couple have no rights of interference in this matter. The changes made with regards to broad principle by the legislature is reduction of statute of limitation from ten years to one year. The start of the limitation, for the parents, is the date when they were informed of the occurrence of the marriage; and for the couple it is from the date that they reach the age of twenty-one.

4. Impediments in marriage contract

These impediments are of two kinds. The main or primary and the secondary or minor impediments. The main impediments are those contracts which not only the Notary public officer refuses to execute, upon being informed of the problems, but even if the contract is executed the problem may result in absolute or relative cancellation of the contract. As an example, if the marriage contract has been concluded in the municipality hall, without the participation of officer of the Notary public records, or without the necessary ceremonies. Such contract falls under the "secrecy" clause of the five categories of mandatory cancellation. Conversely, the minor impediments, if discovered after the marriage contract has been concluded, will have no effect on credibility and legitimacy of transaction. For example a soldier is required to obtain permission to marry from his superior military rank. If the marriage is officiated without such permission such discrepancy will not result in filing a complaint, requesting contract cancellation. If, however, the officer of the Notary and record had become aware of the problem he would have stopped the ceremonies. Also the absence of marriage notice and posting it on the premises of municipality building is considered a minor impediment and has no effect on the outcome after the marriage contract has been executed.

5. Financial relationships of man and wife

The financial affairs of man and wife in French civil law are governed by a special agreement[20]. To regulate such financial relationships, the law has made provisions in four ways. Any of these methods or an alternative that can mutually be satisfactory to both parties of contract and are based on certain conditions- as detailed below- can be adopted.

i) *Shared or Joint wealth*

Here, there are three different sub-categories, distinct from one another. Husband's personal wealth, wife's personal wealth and joint wealth belonging to married couple. After the dissolution of marriage (either through divorce or by death of either party) joint wealth will be distributed equally between the man and woman if divorced; otherwise among the respective survivors. The management of all three classes of funds rests with the husband.

ii) *Segregated wealth*

Since there is no shared wealth each party is the sole owner *and* manager of his or her funds.

iii) *Dowry*

Here, again, there is no shared wealth and that of man and wife is segregated. In particular, the wife's wealth is not transferable at all and it cannot be attached by creditors. The management of this fund is also handled by the husband.

iv) *Unshared wealth*

In this case the wealth of man and wife is segregated and there is no joint funding, but contrary to the case (ii) the management of wife's fund is also controlled by the husband.

In sort, the difference between the wealth being shared and unshared is the absence of joint wealth. They both differ from dowry method with respect to non-transferability and non-attach-ability of wife's wealth. The case of Segregated wealth is unique in that the husband has no control over the funds. Among all four categories the category of joint wealth is most appropriate from legislature's point of view and it is in harmony with general thoughts and customs and traditions of most people, so much that unless the parties expressly state a category other than joint wealth, by default the category of joint wealth will be assumed.

Additional notes

In the past, the method of "shared or joint wealth", in its present form, was predominantly practiced in southern provinces of France, but in the northern region of France the category of method of dowry was more popular. The reason for this difference between the two adopted methods in south and north of France is that in the past Roman laws in the south and German customs and tradition in the north, were dominant[21].

The financial agreement of man and wife like the marriage contract is considered a ceremonial affair and follows certain rules. Similar to marriage contract the financial agreement must be notarized to become effective. It should also be drawn up in the office of Notary public and in the presence of the chief of Notary public. It should be further noted that financial agreement is always prepared prior to marriage ceremony. As explained before, the law makes the determination that the category of joint or shared wealth is the "default" financial agreement. It needs no reminder that in the event the marriage contract is voided or cancelled, the financial agreement, as its function, will also be cancelled or voided.

On July 10th 1850 a law (of Walt) was enacted requiring the official publication of a notice of financial agreements between the married parties, advertised for public information. Prior to that the law of commerce had made this matter compulsory as part of marriage contract for all merchants, but its extension to public at large began from 1850. According to this law the couple must declare to Notary office of Official Records whether or not they had concluded a financial agreement and if so the method that was adopted. If affirmative the written document attested by Notary public had to be presented; otherwise the method of Shared Wealth would apply and any documents to the contrary would not be accepted by court. At any rate, the officer of Notary office of Official Records would make a note of the couple's declared financial agreement method and attach the document to marriage contract and since the details of that document would be published in the official gazette, the third party would become aware of how the financial agreement was structured and would, for example, not engage in any transactions his interests were not served.

Regarding the financial contract of the man and wife the lawmaker has considered two important principles, both of which are generally influential and effective.

i) *Freedom of determination* allows a married couple to act free. In this special case, it presupposes that making a transaction regarding any exchange is absolutely a free act. The law does not interfere in financial arrangements between man and wife, unless no particular arrangement exists between them. Therefore the effective agent is the determination of man and wife; nevertheless, freedom of resolution is limited to cases where the agreement does not clash with public orders and the community's good behavior. This limitation is an interpretation of another basic premise which is embedded in most transactions. Articles 1388 and the subsequent ones prevent any clashes between the financial agreement and public orders and good behavior, as follows:

i$_1$) Husband and wife cannot conclude any agreements whose contents are in variance with the husbandry rights as well as fatherly rights of husband. As observed before, superiority of man over woman and the authorities of husbandry and fatherly of man is considered as those of public orders hence unshakeable from the viewpoint of lawmakers.

i$_2$) Article 1389 prescribes that financial agreement cannot guarantee changes taking place in the inheritance rules because those rules that must be indicated in the will on occasion, and *changeable* by the surviving family members, and always, the last determination of the deceased remain valid. Since the financial agreement for the purpose of protecting the third party's interest is *unchangeable* it cannot include the legally changeable inheritance rules.

i₃) Article 1390 the law prescribes that neither the husband nor the wife, nor the head of Notary public has the right to adapt the rules of financial agreement to the local conditions. This article, which today has no application, was enacted to unify previously varied rules which governed the financial agreements based on local customs and habits in various parts of France. Introduction of this article unified these various customs and habits in an effort to maintain a unified set of rules applicable throughout the country.

The understanding of what has been discussed about basic freedom of determination is that the couple can, by observing the above three conditions, choose any method that suits their situation; whether it is a mix of the different methods incorporated into a national law, or a method specific to the law of a foreign land.

ii) Invariability of the financial agreement- Article 1391 prescribes that financial agreement of marriage after the wedding ceremonies have taken place and the marriage contract has been officially concluded cannot be subjected to any kind of changes (this rule at the same time, restricts the principle of freedom of determination). The law, by citing this principle, protects the interest of the wife and the third parties because it is possible that during the married life the wife is influenced by her husband causing the contract, which was originally to her advantage, be changed to her disadvantage. Regarding the third party it is possible for a man and wife to conspire and change some clauses of their agreement which in fact would have been used as collateral for the wife's transactions with third parties. The changes could cause unfavorable or disadvantageous consequences for third party. Against this general rule, the following two special cases, however, allow the possibility of changes to be made in the financial agreement after the wedding.

ii$_1$) In the event that there is a cause for relative or absolute cancellation of marriage contract the court on the request of prosecutor or interested parties will cancel the contract. Clearly, if man and wife do *not* arrive at an alternative method for their financial agreement, their agreement is, by default, considered to be the method of Shared Wealth.

ii$_2$) In the event that the wife believes her wealth is in danger of being lost by her husband's carelessness she can petition the court to cancel the adopted method and instead apply the method of Segregated Wealth. Of course both changing the agreement from Shared Wealth and replacing it with Segregated Wealth require ruling from the court which will be immediately transmitted to interested parties.

It is possible that the marriage contract upon which the financial agreement is drawn, does not materialize at all in which case the agreement should be immaterial. According to the procedure adopted by French Jurisprudence in the case of cancellation of contract, those parts of articles that have no relevance to marriage are retained. For example, the man had admitted his fatherhood to a son resulting from their illegitimate relationship between them before; or one of the parties has admitted his or her debt to another. These statements since they are recorded as official documents will remain enforced.

The particulars of each of the four methods of financial contracts related to marriage, as foreseen by the law, are detailed below.

a) Method of shared wealth
This official and legal method is a recognized practice in France, Belgium and the Netherlands. Although this is the most commonly used method, the wealthy families show little interest in it and it therefore,

almost exclusively, reserved for middle or income families. The main criticism is due to extraordinary power given to the husband covering the management. Specifically, investing and sale of wife's wealth, all entrusted to husband have made this model unattractive.

The only provision for offsetting this deficiency, as viewed by lawmaker, is that in return for the vast power given by wife to her husband she can refuse to accept her portion of the wealth (profit or loss) and leave any goodness or misdeed to her husband. This option is exercised at the time of cancellation of the shared arrangement, which can take place during the married period, by petitioning the court by either spouse, or by ending the marriage through divorce or death of either spouse. The husband, however, as an executive and manager is always forced to accept the entire joint assets against all the liabilities, caused by his actions.

This probability that the wife may take advantage of her right of refusal and direct all the liabilities of Shared Wealth to her husband at the time of cancellation of agreement may be a cause for husband not to take advantage of his position of power and restrain from wasting the shared assets. This assumption, however, is in fact false. It can not protect the wife's wealth from mismanagement ; it can only make it possible to protect her from future additional losses.

The Capital of Shared Wealth
Because at the time French Civil Code were compiled (1804) the liquid assets did not enjoy the importance of today and were not considered as valuable instrument as they are today, the article 1401 prescribes that the liquid assets which the couple would possess while married including future gains will be part of the Shared Capital. The Civil Laws of the Netherlands name this provision as General Shared Capital and the area that it covers is significantly larger that its counterpart in France, because in Holland all liquid and illiquid assets both prior and after marriage are generally interpreted as Shared Wealth and as a result no *private* fund remains for anyone.

According to French Civil Code, since marriage is considered to be the unification of life and unification of profit and since man and wife must work together, article 1403 prescribes that any illiquid asset that man and wife earn, other than personal gifts during their married life, will be counted as shared asset. According to this all the illiquid assets that they possess on the day of marriage as well as those they later receive as settlement or gift or inheritance would be personal asset because they were not earned as joint income. If however, the donor instead of individually, donate jointly then that asset is part of "joint asset". If either spouse trades his or her illiquid asset to another the new illiquid asset will also be considered private asset provided there is no net gain. If there is significant net loss paid out of the Shared Wealth, the new illiquid asset will belong to the "joint asset". The respective spouse will then be credited from the Shared Wealth the amount equivalent to the value of the old illiquid asset. Any payment against such credit to the spouse will be made at the time of liquidation of Shared Wealth and final settlement.

With regards to exchanged gifts given by parents or grand parents, in the form of illiquid asset, bestowed to either spouse, it could be considered as part of Shared Wealth as per general rule. Yet, since there is a possibility this same asset could later be transferred as inheritance to the above-mentioned spouse, it will be treated under private asset and will not be relevant to Shared Wealth.

Another case that may arise in this regard, is that the wife has sold her own private property, authorized by her husband, but she plans to acquire another property with its sale proceeds. Since the property's sale takes place during the married life and it is not (obtained for) free (as a gift,... etc.) it should be incorporated in the Shared Wealth in accordance with the rule; on the other hand the replacement is another property belonging to the wife, the sale proceeds of which, should be her private asset. The law confirms the latter reasoning and since the proceed of sale of property is legally collected by the husband as the financial director of the family and it is possible that he would use it for other purposes, the wife has the right to insist in putting a clause in the sale document that the purchaser is required to protect and supervise the property sale value until it is applied for purchase of new property. In this case the purchaser delivers the funds to the safe deposit designated by the Notary office of records to be used by the husband to pay towards the purchase of new property.

Increase or decrease of capital of Shared Wealth
In addition to what the law has provided, based on freedom of determination the married couple can specify items regarding the addition or reduction of capital to their Shared Wealth in their financial agreement. For addition they can agree that all of their illiquid wealth whether from the past or future should be incorporated into the Shared Wealth, or to even include a property that is legally a private one, or instead of the property an under valued (estimated) price to be added to the Shared Wealth in which case the property remains in the possession of the spouse, but is used as collateral against the borrowed funds by the husband.

As for the reduction of capital, which presently is more often used, the married couple may agree that their liquid assets be interpreted as illiquid. This means the liquid assets that had resulted as earned income after the marriage would remain in the Shared Wealth and the rest would become private asset to spouses. The reason for this view, as observed before, is that since the 19th century the worth of liquid assets such as corporate stocks, traded securities and government bonds have become common knowledge. On the other hand, the illiquid assets have lost their appeal since the Civil Code were compiled. Now as a result of re-allocation of assets, the husband could allocate all of his liquid assets as capital in the "Shared Wealth" while all of his wife's assets, comprising illiquid assets, before her wedding, and her properties obtained through gift or inheritance later on can be kept by herself, i.e., as private. This will allow her less valued liquid assets be co-mingled with much more impressive liquid assets of her husband. This arrangement with the consent of the wife, therefore, would make it fair to treat the liquid and illiquid assets alike.

Management of Real-estate asset of Shared Wealth
In accordance with article 1421 the husband has the right to solely manage the Shared Wealth, which includes selling and using the asset as collateral, for borrowing or transferring in any other form which he sees fit. The rights of husband in managing and transferring assets derive from his being the head of the family and his superiority and supremacy, which as viewed by law is a component of general arrangements in a society.

According to the law enacted on 13th of July 1907, one other kind of separate wealth is assumed for woman which is still part of the capital of Shared Wealth as far as ownership is concerned. The law specifies that the woman's income is under her own control and sh alone is empowered with respect to authority, directing, possession and savings. The proviso is, however, it must be spent towards the necessary expenses of the household. Whatever the wife could save from this income source will then be her private capital upon dissolution of the Shared Wealth and the husband will have no rights on such funds.

The lawmaker has provided a very effective tool to control the seemingly vast and extraordinary authority given to the man who could otherwise jeopardize the wife's entire wealth by incurring significant losses. The law stipulates that the wife has the right to take up a forcible mortgage of not only all the assets of Shared Wealth, but also those of private wealth of her husband. If at the cancellation of marriage or dissolution of Shared Wealth[22] the wife is owed by her husband she has the right to place a lien against any assets belonging to Shared Wealth or that of her husband's private wealth, irrespective of possession at the time, in order to secure her claim. This tool serves as a deterrent, because the future creditors become aware of such legal right of the wife and as such will demand a waiver or

consent written and signed by the wife before conducting any transactions with the husband . Accordingly, the husband will have to
consult with his wife on any transactions and secure her consent.
Further, article 1422 denies the husband's right of giving any gifts in
the form of illiquid assets belonging to Shared Wealth. The matter of
whether the husband can give such gifts with the consent of the wife,
however, is a subject for discussion. In the judicial doctrine no fixed
procedure has been adopted. If the husband wants to make a will
regarding the Shared Wealth he can only do so for his own one-half
share. The wife has the exact position even without her husband's
permission.

Managing of Wife's private assets

The article 1428 has given the right, as well as duty, of handling all
wife's private assets to the husband, but at the same time any transactions with regards to liquid[23] or illiquid assets of wife, outside the definition of "managing" assets is not possible by the husband alone and it
requires the wife's signed agreement. In reality, it can be stated that as
a general rule the wife herself becomes the transferee, albeit with the
consent of the husband. The above article stipulates that the husband
will be responsible for any embezzlement resulting from his negligence
or error with regards to his wife's assets.

Although as it has repeated before that wife's assets are managed by
the husband, it should be noted that the husband's authorities in this
affair is considerably less than his power over the Shared Wealth and, of
course, his own private assets. One of the noticeable action in handling
the wife's assets is leasing her real estates. In this regard, the period of
lease must not exceed nine years and if so it must be a period divis-
ible by nine. As a result at anytime that during any of such periods the
"Shared Wealth" is dissolved the wife must honor the lease contract
only until the end of related nine years; at the end of which she can cancel the remaining nine- year period.

Liabilities of Shared Wealth

As in the case of assets the law has made distinctions between liquid and illiquid asset each before and after the wedding. The law also makes distinctions regarding liabilities as follows:

i) Liabilities prior to wedding- As mentioned before, regarding the capital of Shared Wealth, only the liquid assets are being shared among all assets belonging to man and wife on the wedding day. For liability also, in order to maintain the balance between asset and liability of Shared Wealth, article 1409 prescribes that the liquid debts carried by the married couple, as of the day of wedding, will become the liability of Shared Wealth.

The noteworthy point is that such balance is artificial, nominal and unreal. The reasoning for this assertion is that although the separation of liquid and illiquid assets is simple, liquid and illiquid debt cannot easily be segregated to cash and hence liquid as well as non cash. Here is an explanation.

Generally, once a consent is legally secured, since it is implicit in the commitment, one can conclude that the commitment takes place at once. For example, if the matter is about commitment of transfer of illiquid asset it can be done immediately; in other words, it is not the act of transaction requiring separate protocol and action, but the issue is the results. It is, however, a different matter if a conditional commitment is made , for example, indicating a properly to be transferred at a specific date, or the commitment to transfer a property whose location to be determined and its boundaries to be identified.

As a result, an illiquid debt is generally non existent. Hence the ruling that *all* debts that the married couple were committed to, before their married life, will be passed on to the Shared Wealth carries little weight.

ii) Liabilities during the married life

All commitments made to the third parties by the husband during the married life of the couple will be concluded by the "Shared Wealth". The creditor has the choice of attaching the husband's private asset or the Shared Wealth, whether the resulting obligation was caused by his managing the private asset or the asset related to Shared Wealth. With regards to the wife's loan and obligations there are three cases to be considered:

- If the obligation is made without the husbands permission, because of her disqualification the transaction is treated as a relative cancellation.

- If the transaction was sanctioned by the court the obligation is valid, but only the wife's private assets is considered the guarantor.

- In the event the transaction was permitted by the husband the creditor can prosecute by attaching the private assets of both man and wife as well as the Shared Wealth.

Therefore even if the husband would like to go along with his wife's transaction to proceed he would generally decline to offer permission and would let the case to go to the court.

Dissolution and Distribution of Shared Wealth

Causes for dissolution- Article 1441 lists the reasons for dissolution as:

- Natural death of either spouse

- Legal death where punishment for committing crime would take away civil and social rights of the individual (not practiced now in French jurisprudence).

- Divorce.

– Physical separation (that is described at length in later section, Divorce).

– Financial separation ordered by the court of law.

Method of distribution- Firstly, the spouses will retrieve exactly whatever they owned, now existing. Secondly, they transfer the funds which is owed to them, by the Shared Wealth as results of various transactions. Among the privileges that the lawmaker has provided for the wife is that she can demand her funds before her husband's.

To retrieve their funds there is a possibility that the spouses differ about the valuation of assets in their Shared Wealth that may result in the referral of case to the court. This could also result in a loss to the third parties (to whom the Shared Wealth owes). Second, if there is a collusion between the spouses in which case the creditors can file a special[24] complaint defending their rights. Third, if the private assets of spouses carry any debts to Shared Wealth they must repay their debts. Fourth, after all accounting procedures the remaining funds will be divided evenly. Fifth, as discussed before, the wife, due to extraordinary rights of man, has the right to refuse her portion of Shared Wealth in the event that the Shared Wealth debt resulting from the husband's obligation exceed its assets. Finally, If the wife accepts the liability of Shared Wealth her portion of liability to creditors is limited to what she has received from that account[25]. This limitation is similar to the extent of debt to which the heirs are committed with regards to what is inherited; the difference being that the heirs must formally ask for their rights, but the wife will automatically and without any formal request will benefit from this protection.

b) Method of separation of wealth

This method is quite rare in practice. In 1898 among 82,346 marriage financial agreements only 2128 (little more than 2%) followed this path which deals with specific cases, for example, a wife who has had a child from her previous marriage. The advantage of this method is twofold. One is the independence that is given to married woman, in relative terms, another is for transparency of the spouses financial positions in case of divorce. As such the societies promoting women's rights try to generalize this method within French Jurisprudence and to particularly apply it to the regions (of France) where the rate of divorce (as per above example) is high. In this method the wealth of spouses are quite distinct and additionally each spouse handles his or her account personally and as observed before, this separation may be in the form of agreement or judicially executed. This type of agreement is the legal form to which man and wife abide before the marriage ceremonies. A judicial separation can also take place in the course of married life. It is usually initiated by the wife requesting financial separation from the court whereupon, the court will make a determination and issues a ruling to protect her wealth.

In any of the two cases the husband has no part in his wife's assets and income, but she must contribute to the required household expenses. In the case of judicial separation the court takes notice of financial standing of the spouses as well as the average household expenses and then specifies the amount of her contribution in the issued ruling. If at anytime the financial conditions of the married couple changes they can, return to the court and, petition the court to adjust the ruling according to then present circumstance.

In the case of contractual separation if no agreement is reached between the spouses regarding woman's share of contribution to household expenses, one-third of woman's income must be allocated to the expenses. Since it is possible that in view of husband position and with respect to wife's wealth, this division of income may appear unfair, in which case, the court will assess the fair share for each spouse. Usually the wife gives one third of her income to her husband; alternatively, if she is in charge of livelihood she will collect from her husband his agreed share of his income. On 19th of

May 1920, French Court of Tribunal recommended such contractual arrangement which would have no legal impediment. In this case if anything is saved from the household expenses in accordance to the law enacted in 13th July 1907 would belong to the wife and would remain under her control.

Limitation of independence and qualification of wife in the method of separation
According to article 1449, firstly, wife can manage her own finances. Secondly, she has the right to transact her liquid assets in any manner she chooses. Thirdly, transfer of illiquid asset is contingent upon the husband's consent or a court order. As the article clearly states law-maker has given freedom of doing any transactions regarding her liquid assets, but transfer of her illiquid assets will depend on her husband's determination.

The rationale for this differentiation is the same topic discussed regarding the extraordinary economic value of illiquid asset in early nineteenth century (the time of compiling of civil code). As noted before, until late 19th century other than illiquid assets, no other attractive wealth products existed and woman's liquid assets were limited to house furnitures. This was partly because of difficulty for woman to part with the necessary means of living furniture and even if she wished to sell any such illiquid assets her husband's permission was required.

Ever since late nineteenth century, however, due to expansion of industry and trade the variety and worth of liquid assets have significantly increased in such a way that an individual could be worth millions in just paper money, in the form of stocks of corporations, bank notes, ... etc.

As such, freedom of woman in transacting her liquid assets could prove to be dangerous for her and her husband. For this reason, the French jurisprudence considered the illiquid asset as the extension of first part, which is the liquid asset in a practical sense, that the woman's independence in liquid asset transaction is valid and that the transaction is *limited* to her financial administration need. For example, the wife can independently spend her farm's rental money for purchase of seeds or other tools and equipment required for farming, but it is not proper for her to execute a significant transaction, unrelated to her administrative need that may change her financial picture, without her husband's permission.

One must note that although article 1449 does not openly reject woman's transfer of properties which do not result in any profit or loss, but with the limitation imposed on her authorities, from the view point of lawmaker and in practice she cannot donate as gift any of her own liquid or illiquid assets without her husband's permission. According to article 215, even based on method of Separation of Wealth, husband's permission was required for woman to lodge a legal complaint. The permission from the husband is not limited to complaints regarding illiquid asset, but it also includes any disputes regarding woman's liquid assets which, by itself, she is supposedly allowed to execute freely.

On the subject of woman being allowed to create any obligation for herself without her husband's permission, although article 1449 is silent, but another article 220 regarding married women's right to commerce, confirms their lack of qualification and because of this the French jurisprudence has prescribed that woman's obligation is enforceable only when the transaction does not exceed the limit that is necessary for administering her financial affair. Therefore, the wife is forbidden to guarantee a third party, or to make a settlement, or to commit to accept a ruling, or to accept an inheritance without her husband's permission.

As noted before, the law enacted on 13th July 1907 allows the woman to spend her earned income independently, waiving many of general regulations. In a similar manner and regarding Separation of Wealth, woman is allowed to sell any and all of her assets, liquid or illiquid and additionally, lodging any complaints related to such wealth without her husband's permission.

c) Method of dowry

The genesis of this method existed in Roman laws. Later, as will be seen, with changes that were necessary for evolution and the transformations that have taken place, in the course of time, this method was accepted by French jurisprudence. The particular characteristic of this method is the division of the wife's wealth to dowry and the non-dowry. The dowry wealth which is administered and utilized by the husband is non-transferable neither by wife, nor by husband, nor jointly and because of inability to transfer these assets the statutory limitation does not apply. Further more, an intermittent possession by non relatives will not constitute ownership. Also, third parties cannot attach and sell these assets as a means to secure their credit.

The non-dowry assets can be both transferred and attached, but these will be administered by the wife herself.

Fixing a measure and a value for each of the two types of the assets depends on mutual agreement between the married couple. Therefore it can be concluded that this method is a combination of two methods of Segregated Wealth and Non-sharing Wealth. The rationale for establishing this method is a deliberate intention for retaining a portion of the family wealth forever. That is why the illiquid assets that come in the form of dowry is absolutely non-transferable.

Advantages of the method of dowry:
The biggest advantage of this method is that the wife and her assets are protected in the best way against the excesses and unbecoming activities of the husband because her illiquid assets are absolutely non transferable and as far as liquid assets, although it is possible to be sold by the husband, but in comparison to the value of illiquid private asset of her husband it may be worth at least the same, and therefore the assets of the wife is preserved. This is due to the right of woman to apply her automatic right of mortgage on her husband's property for claim against the equivalent of her portion of liquid asset that her husband had wasted.

Even in this method of dowry, contrary to other three methods (Shared wealth, Segregated Wealth and Non-shared wealth) in accordance to French Jurisprudence she cannot forego her rights of applying forced mortgage, but if the husband does not possess any illiquid assets the wife will have no recourse to recover her loss and of course in such case she will not adopt this method.

Another advantage of this method, that is highly significant in its own right, is that the wife's income from dowry assets are also non-transferable and cannot be attached by creditors in accordance with accepted opinions in the judicial principle, to the extent that is necessary for living expenses. As such the method of dowry is more advantageous than Shared Wealth where the husband can transfer his wife's income -derived from her assets, with no regards for household expenses, but in the case of dowry he is forced to take the living expenses into account.

One of the deficiencies observed here is the suspicion of the husband's morality, because according to this method, and contrary to general perception of marriage and the unity of both parties interests, the wealth and income of each party is segregated and further, the wife's wealth is intensely protected against the husband's possessions for administering the assets. Another fault is that from economic point of view, woman is not allowed to utilize her assets and the husband cannot take advantage of his wife's credit worthiness resulted from her wealth. Additionally, he is not allowed to dispose of his own illiquid assets or mortgage it because his wife has the first right of mortgage and since she cannot forego that option the husband cannot find a buyer for his property. Also, the third parties may incur damages in any transaction due to potential collusion of man and wife. The only remedy that is practiced for fixing these deficiencies is to include a clause in the financial agreement between the married couple, in which the wife allows her husband to sell her dowry assets, liquid or illiquid, if necessary provided the husband is obligated to replace and deliver the assets upon his wife's demand.

Based on the above-mentioned deficiencies the application of the dowry method is decreased and is now limited to some remote areas such as Montpelier and Normandy.

Historical background:
Roman laws recognized husband's full authority over his wife's dowry. Gradually, however, the area of authority became smaller until Justinian period which stripped the husband from the right of transfer or mortgage of the wife's dowry; not even with his wife's consent. If he had wasted his wife's asset, contrary to the norm, he would have to return the replacement of her assets at the time of separation of wealth or dissolution of marriage contract. The old version of French laws reflected the identical form of this and additionally, French Courts clearly had ruled that the wife had the right of ownership to her dowry. Accordingly, French Civil Code followed and re-affirmed the same ruling. Therefore the owner of dowry is recognized to be the wife only and the husband had the right to administer the affairs as related to such assets and any income derived from the assets which can be used for the family's necessary expenses.

Clearly, the right to administer is inclusive of all the authorities that are required for proper asset management and as a result, he can personally lodge any complaints regarding the assets and he can further, as explained in previous section, transfer the liquid asset of his wife's dowry, but he had to compensate his wife with its replacement or its equivalent cash value. The reason for such authority is:

First, since the husband has taken possession of his wife's liquid assets, and as such, is recognized as owner of the liquid assets; therefore he has the right to sell those assets. Second, since the husband can, as part of his administrative operations, transfer or exchange the documents and demand notes of her liquid assets including the right to trade her corporate stocks and financial-instruments. Third, since the trading of liquid assets are alike, selling of physical, but liquid assets, such as furnitures, etc., would also be allowed.

Change of management:
The dowry method has also contains similar features detailed under "Shared Wealth," that is, the right of wife to petition the court to dislodge her husband from his right of administering her dowry assets, due to his improper administration and operation, and to grant her the same. In this case, the right of administering and utilization of income derived from the assets will belong solely to the wife, and at the same time the rules that apply in this method for protection of her wealth remains in place albeit with some minor changes. All authorities needed for administering her assets are given to her to collect all her income derived from her assets, and as in the method of Separation of Wealth, to contribute towards household expenses. For lodging a complaint, however, she would need her husband's permission which in case of his refusal she may petition the court.

Separation of the dowry from non-dowry assets:
In the event of wresting the right of administration from the husband, the dowry assets still remain non-transferable and cannot be attached by creditors. In fact the liquid dowry assets also become non-transferable; that is because during the husband's administration, the wife could not transfer by herself either. The income of dowry assets will also be added to the assets; any gifts or inheritance if given to her will also become part of her dowry. Only the advantage of "inapplicability of statute of limitation" regarding the dowry asset is no longer in effect after the separation takes place (that is, the statute of limitation is now applicable to dowry assets).

It is worth noting that the inability of attaching the wife's dowry assets only applies to creditors who have had financial transactions with her *after* her marriage; otherwise the creditors would have assumed that her assets were transferable and attachable as they were before her marriage and hence would collect what they were owed.

In conclusion one should note that regarding the basic premise of non-transferability and non attach-ability of woman's dowry, there are exceptions for which the lawmakers have enacted (for particularly good intention). For example, if someone has incurred losses due to her misdemeanor, or similar offense they can at the time of lodging complaint attach her dowry whereupon if proven that the person is entitled to an award the proceeds of the assets will be collected. Another exception is the law enacted on nineteen of March 1919 for the interest of public welfare and charities, specifically for encouraging and facilitating reproduction and nurturing of the orphaned children, a casualty of First World War. Here, the wife could sell her illiquid assets with her husband's permission, or through a court order if he refused, provided she had no children and that she was over forty five years of age. Apparently the age factor indicated her being excluded from reproductivity.

d) Method of non-sharing
This method, as in the case of Separation of Wealth, stipulates that the wealth of man is separated from that of wife; and there is no common wealth, but contrary to the method of Separation of Wealth the management of the wife's wealth is vested with the husband and transfer of assets for each party follows the general rules as prescribed by law. This method has a limited application in France, but in Germany it is interpreted as Method of General Law in accordance with civil law compiled in 1900.

Since through this method, administering of woman's wealth and its income are controlled by her husband, he is also responsible for the household expenses, using the income of his own private wealth as well as his wife's wealth and income. Accordingly, any savings if it exists will belong to the husband. As for the wife's qualification this method does not allow her to engage in any legal transaction without the permission of her husband. She can, as noted before, in accordance to ruling of 13ᵗʰ July 1907, utilize the income of her own assets and spend it as necessary for household expenses. Any savings if possible will be hers which she could possess and manage.

An overview of comparison between Islam's laws and that of the European whose most detailed and comprehensive version would be French Civil Code can be viewed that contrary to some perception, the boundaries of rights of woman-specially for the married woman-in Islam's Sharia is many times broader than her freedom of executing legal transactions and many times more expanded in utilization of her wealth and it certainly makes far less demand with lighter duty as compared with western societies.

Highlights

1. Financial affair: The married woman is required to contribute to the household expenses. The three methods of financial agreement require that the entire income of the wife be controlled by the husband.

2. Financial risk: Even with certain safeguards incorporated into civil laws, woman's entire wealth is in danger of being wasted or abused by the husband.

3. Dependency: Woman is treated just like a child in need of guardian to watch and supervise her. Woman in all aspects of social life, except drawing a will, is dependent on her husband's will and remains under his control. Married woman for even the least important legal matter needs her husband's consent.

4. Islam's Sharia prescribes that her income and wealth is no one's business except hers and in all legal transactions. she is fully authorized to make legal transaction with complete qualification vested in her alone and she is not bound to sharing of the household expenses.

CHAPTER THREE
Polygamy

This subject both socially and legally deserves full attention. Prior to Islam's Sharia, the customs allowed man to marry more than one woman if he was capable and observant of certain conditions. The European laws not only reject this act, but they consider it a public disorder and immoral. They believe that committing such act would injure the sensitivity and general feelings of civilized nations. Furthermore, such detestable and abominable acts are classified as slave trading.

The issue of legal relationships of citizens of a nation with a foreign government, or the people of a foreign nation is often a matter of interest in the field of international law. A foreign national, in general, is admitted to reside in another country who in accordance to his national identity, would be subject to legal regulations of his own country and hence exempt from the laws and regulations of the host country in which he resides.

For example, a Frenchman residing in Iran is considered "of legal age" before the Iranian court when in accordance to French laws he has reached the required legal age (completed twenty- first year) for all personal status such as marriage, inheritance, etc. The only observable exception would be the problem of conflict with public order and good morals.

Perpetrating acts that in view of a nation is unanimously abominable and disagreeable offends public sensitivities of that nation. Therefore, although the perpetrator's action is part of his personal status, and according to his national laws, he is allowed to do so, he cannot do the same in the foreign land.

For example, assuming the purchase of a slave in country A, was per- mitted. The citizen of that country if residing in a another country B, that does not allow to trade slave, cannot do so and refer the com- plaints brought against him, to the courts of his country of origin. That is because the society (of the country B of his domicile) considers the committed act contrary to its good morals and as such, does not allow it to become a subject of discussion in his court. The issue of polygamy is viewed by European laws as this kind of example.

In this section the origins and reasons for obscenity and indecency of this practice from the view point of western lawmakers and the rationale for its acceptance by Islam's Sharia are fully explored.

The criticism
In the beginning of this journey it appears that the growth and improve- ment of woman's position in the society along with her legal and social prestige, both acknowledged today, command that a man must not take more than one woman as his wife. This is because:

i) The woman's merit in the society is by no means less than the man and the weakness which is still exhibited in her physical and mental condition relative to that of man is caused by deficiency of nurturing and lack of attention. It is quite possible that she would have otherwise developed her analytical and moral traits.

ii) It is experimentally proven that the best way to promote woman's worth and to develop her capabilities is the observance of respect, accolade of her status, inspiring her soul for acquiring self respect, chastity and magnanimity. Based on this observation, one must refrain from any insults and discourtesy towards woman's position of respect. Any insult and humiliation will cause the bright flame of woman's honor and chastity to extinguish in her soul.

iii) Allowing a man to take two, three or four wives can be interpreted as valuing several women the same as one man which is a big humiliation to woman's social ranking and esteemed position. It will cause a general deterioration and lowering of morals and woman's declining morale in particular.

iv) Considering the sense of jealousy and competition that rules human-kind, polygamy would create intense hatred and grudge among the wives, the relatives and their families as well as causing mischief-makings and discord among the children of different wives.

v) Since the strongest factor in advancement and progress in any group is harmony and concord and assisting one another, in the case of polygamy discord and negativity of one group against another prevents social development and progress of families making them inherently weak as the foundation of society. This is the judgement of those against polygamy and endorse the "one-wife" (marriage) only.

The explanation
From the viewpoint of this writer; [1] in the above-mentioned statements and judgement, the attention to one basic point has been neglected. Although, the reasoning appears to be sound and logical it will not be consistent with reality of the essence of things as explained below.

185

First, one has to note the population distribution in terms of male and female and which sex is in majority. If there is a quantitative equality between the two sexes the above-mentioned logic is correct and practical and polygamy should not be practiced at all, but otherwise polygamy should be, at least theoretically, allowed because if no man can have more than one wife, naturally the remaining woman population will remain unmarried.

On the one hand the need of a man and a woman to associate with one another and interest in marriage is a natural matter and aside from woman's livelihood which is usually guaranteed by her man, the woman is in need of a husband and to satisfy herself of kind feelings is enamored to be an object of existing in a man's mind. A law which is enacted without caring for human natural needs and feelings and does not correspond to the circumstances cannot be enforced and will not endure. The dogmatic and irrational rules will not prevent the unmarried women from inclination and developing a relation with married men. As a result, every man has one official wife and several unofficial illegitimate wives.

There are apparently two moral and social deficiencies applicable to polygamy.

The primary concern is that it humiliates the woman's status, making her insignificant and lessens her worth as compared to a man. One wonders what would happen to the merit and esteem of a woman who secretly and illegitimately develops relationship with a married man surrendering her honor, chastity, prestige and attribute, in secret, fearing the illegitimate relationship if exposed. Such act will certainly stain her standing and honor and at the end nothing would be left of her moral distinction and pride.

As for the hatred and grudge among the wives and their relations to each other, there should be no difference between polygamy and the illegitimate relationship of married man. In the case of illegitimate relationship, the legal wife of the man, the children and relatives naturally will resent and may hate the woman who shares their father intimate relationship, since no matter how secret the relation is kept ultimately it will become apparent at some point, one way or another.

The other concern, that should be addressed is the subject of reproduction. The issue revolves around additional children which is actually a positive sign, considering the attention given in the industrial nations[2] in recent years towards increasing the newborns, and the need for increase in those countries' population; this, in fact, is one of the advantages of polygamy. There should be no doubt that in the event that the female population exceeds that of male, polygamy will increase the number of newborns many times more than just one married couple. The reason being that fewer men are available for marriage and reproducing. It should also be noted that normally illegitimate relationships rarely result in reproducing and even if a child is produced there will be, in addition to social stigma, complications and difficulties regarding minor offense and judicial matters.

Finally, a woman who considers herself an equal partner with her husband at all levels and enjoys no less privileges than her husband would naturally possess the moral merits and self accomplishments that prepare her to qualify for her rightful status and respect. This is the most powerful weapon for the woman to withstand any perceived humiliation or loss of respect.

The choices

Based on the above explanations, declaring polygamy in an absolute sense and without regards to particular circumstances and external factors is erroneous. It cannot be justified to generally brand it as obscene and immoral, in the name of defending women's rights and prestige. Instead this matter should be studied in view of the environment, society and special period (of time and age). To start, the ratio of male to female of population in a society (or nation) should be noted. It is common knowledge that generally there are more women than men worldwide and as such, under certain conditions and particular choices, polygamy may have an application; otherwise the currency of indecency and prostitution will markedly increase and the number of newborns will drop in that particular society or nation. Of course it is not intended to claim that the only factor for increased prostitution within a nation where there are more women than men is because of prevention of polygamy and that one necessitates another. No, that is not so. Rather there are other influencing and contributing factors that affect the outcome, but it is with certainty that by denying polygamy even the thought of preventing prostitution is impossible because in such case the men and women will be the driving force, by their nature, in promoting it. Woman's motivation is the natural desire of having relationship with man; and for man, as explained before, his motives are derived from a famous proverb that Man's desire increases for anything that he is prohibited from. As a possible means of preventing man from any disposition towards prostitution a sufficiently wealthy man, author argues, should be permitted to marry more than one woman. Just to have this permit and its possible use will satisfy his appetite for lust and would make him committed to moral standards.

The constraints

The first condition for permitting polygamy, according to Islam's teaching, is the physical and financial health of the man in such a way that he would guarantee the living expenses and satisfy all the women needs as well as the children, sufficiently. While it is true that Islam's Sharia allows a man, based on circumstances, historical backgrounds, the necessity of reproducing newborns and preventing prostitution to marry up-to four wives; such permission is contingent upon execution of full extent of justice and observance of fairness and impartiality. The permit to a man who may be suspected of not being able to treat two women or more equally is denied. Justice is clearly defined to treat wives equally at all emotional levels, including hearty inclination and a sense of belonging. It can be said, therefore, that Islam has allowed polygamy in a nominal term, but its practical use is almost in abeyance[3].

Additionally, it should be noted that introducing Islam's Sharia took place when the prevailing rules and habits in the world at the time, not only permitted men taking unlimited wives, but in principle the right of a woman as a person was not recognized and, as it was noted before, woman was thought of being man's "shadow" making her a submissive follower. In China, according to the law, a man could have as many as one hundred and thirty wives. In Judaism, marrying up to several hundred women were sanctioned with impunity. Islam, while bestowing independence and dignity to woman, limited the number of wives in polygamy (to four) and made its applicability contingent upon almost impossible or extraordinarily difficult conditions. Many early Muslims already married to more than four wives[4] did in fact comply with the new directive.

Conclusion

It is apparent that based on the above analysis, the topic of polygamy in view of Islam and Sharia, in general, and as practiced in Muslim countries should not be subject to criticism. It is also not inconsistent with civility and humanity as it appears to westerners. A statement published in "Religions of the World" sums up this topic neatly.

"Islam on the matter of marriage has exceeded the boundary of being mindful of women's rights and has imposed and obligated the man to every kind of observances. Polygamy, irrespective of its necessity and benefits belongs to a time of Happening of Islam and limited the Arabs unbounded and numerous wives to four and made it contingent upon the fair treatment of the women based on equality and justice. Justice includes evenly heart-felt affection".

Additionally, Issac Tiller, in one of his sermons in the gathering of all churches in Germany, has said:

"It is true that Christians apparently do not take more than one wife, but we all know that behind the hidden walls they maintain shameful relationships with several women".

CHAPTER FOUR
Social view of marriage

This chapter is devoted to a short discussion focusing on critical social issues leading to formation of family; that is, a foundation for a civil societies and, ultimately, nations.

It is well known that in every corner of the world there are young people who prefer a care-free and bachelor life to a committed married life. Such people opt for wasting their money on indulgences and frivolous amusements, move frequently from one place to another to escape boredom instead of what could have been an alternative choice of establishing a family through reproducing and building a healthy foundation for their society.

The necessity of married life from the point of view of society and its benefits as well as its advantages outcome over bachelorhood are probably not hidden from everyone including the youth. There should not be the least bit of doubt that marriage, and as a result, the reproduction would be the prime driving force behind the growth and the strength of any sound society. The problem is that man, in principle, is influenced by selfishness and narcism, perceiving that the world revolves around him alone. He is not prepared to sacrifice his pleasure for the comfort of the others. The selfishness does not provide the opportunity to adhere to moral teachings and similar attributes. The young bachelors think that by not being tied to wife and children they would enjoy every kind of peace and comfort and tranquility they desire. The mere disengagement and being unconcerned with other people's affairs, whether at work or at home, will not make them free to choose their style of living and free to seek pleasure and physical attraction forever. That accepting the responsibility of one's family expenses, nurturing the children and managing the family affair will invite unnecessary annoyance is a false belief.

The youth questions the wisdom of an imaginary promise that unquantified and vague benefit may result from years of pain and toil. Furthermore one has to forego his present freedom and peace of mind, accepting the hardship of a married life.

Everyone single man imagines his individual duty of commitment to marriage by itself does not affect the society and such social responsibility can be carried out by others. They are unaware of the fact that if each and every individual thinks that his contribution does not count the entire youth generation, of the society, will go on believing that no one needs to be responsible for his civic duty.

The author is of the opinion that in promoting charity and encouraging praiseworthy motivation for achieving the desired result, one must first demonstrate the personal benefit and advantage of the action which the person would gain as direct beneficiary. The benefits of this important matter, for every married youth is described below.

Marriage: As viewed by an individual
It should be noted that nature possesses extremely firm and everlasting means and rules such that they never waver; and no beings will be

excepted from its inclusiveness and generality. Life, growth, evolution and lasting of all kinds and classes of beings will adhere to a series of general rules that last forever and exist everywhere and are invariable for everyone. Humankind is also, as in other types and classes of creatures, are forced to follow the invariable ways of creation because violating these laws will result in lawbreaker's loss.

A summary reference to various classes of creatures or beings, will identify this tradition of unavoidability and inevitability. In the tradition of creation, the flawless and ideal perfection the goal for any being is to struggle with death and ensure its existence, but eternity is not possible because in the material world the matter is not unlimited and boundless. A being tries to maintain its eternal existence of its kind by prototyping with guaranteed face of its kind.

The perfection of the seed of wheat, corn and lentil, etc. is accomplished through reproduction of its own kind; by maintaining its worldly kind it will not be subjected to annihilation in its battle with natural causes. To achieve this goal it has to overcome intense difficulties and must make significant sacrifices.

After the seed is buried underground, this being gives up its existence; its being is annihilated and is surrendered to the goodness of growth and development of another being. By doing so it looks forward to the occasion that its seed-like being will rise and grow out of the earth with a superior quality and nobility, covered with green skin, and finally asserting itself in the world of vegetation.

A grain of wheat which, not long ago, was a solid element, lacking the power of nourishment and growth, is now a member of advance class of vegetation, being fed by the means of nature and growing daily to eventually becoming the carrier of one hundred of its wheat grain-kind, left as his memorial as it annihilates. Now, each grain repeats the process one thousand fold maintaining its prototype kind. Had the grain of wheat remained in the store at resting position and idlic state, it could have never been able to be nourished and grow and as a result would have been unable to achieve its perfected being.

A branch of a green weed for the love of growing and progress surrenders itself to the sheep's sharp teeth and as a result of this sacrifice replaces its plain green cover of vegetation with the more meaningful cover of an animal. A vegetable which had no sense and movement before making its sacrifice and humiliation, now has joined the class of sheep; it now enjoys having animal's great advantages. The sheep also, after being slaughtered, its flesh becomes ground meat under the powerful gears of rotary machine, prepared for the next stage of growth and development. It submits itself to be annihilated, sacrificing itself as food for human. The being has achieved the capability and qualification that would transform itself to make a fine liquid and send it as human blood which circulates through the brain, the central command and manifestation of higher thinkings of humankind.

A sesame seed which probably occupies and therefore controls, less than one cubic millimeter of space, thanks to pressurizer, is converted to a fine oil; that is, the embedded oil is extracted by pressing after being ignited and then converted from a black seed to a clear particle in the form of light, encompassing the entire space that surrounds it. The small dark spots within the space are swallowed making them lighted. These examples demonstrate the miraculous effects of pain and stress. Here is a quote from *Alfred de Mousse*, the French poet:

"Nothing will make a man great as a great pain does[1]".

An unmarried man fearing the preoccupation with wife and children as well as the fear for upsetting his desire for comfort and self indulgence, will lack any motivation for growth and advancement. A famous saying states: "The eyes and ears that have not experienced pain by baby's cries in the middle of night and have not lost sleep over it; a heart that in the process of nurturing a child has not suffered from various disagreeable and troublesome events and a mind that has not adapted to dealing with handling wife and children has not reached maturity. Such a man even at his old age has not grown up."

Rumi:

A dog is not for hunting if it wears no collar;
the un-refined un-polished one is noting but disingenuous.
When you are hurtful of all enmities;
free you become of all resentments.

After daily chores and laboring everyday hardship, where would an unmarried man go and with whom would he be acquainted? For his recreation and relaxation of soul and body, he will find no entertainment and enjoyment that is lasting, or durable; additionally he is not immune from critical and harmful consequences of indulgences. The only noble and honorable sociable hobby that can make a man amused and happy throughout his life is nurturing healthy and strong children who ultimately award their parents with pride and joy. Those who have never experienced their fathers enjoyment, are unaware of the kind of affection of a child and are incapable of appreciating it. This spiritual and heavenly affection is so delicious, pure and far from materialistic bias, one hour of which will easily offset all the hardship and inconveniences of time spent for nurturing of children and the associated mental stress.

Quoting Gustave *Le Bonne*, the French social scientist, "the only corner (of the world) that can turn the sad and depressed state of mind of a man into happiness, and erase all fatigue and daily unfavorables from his memory is the family home". This is true because it is the place that all members and individuals share all their positive physical and mental experiences and such unity of common interest prevents each one of them from any prevarication and discords among them. The honor and material resource of husband will be a cause for the wife's dignity and peace of mind and his financial resources and standing will belong to the children.

In summary everyone man or woman young or old will share everything with each other and as such there is no discord or double dealing among them and when there is no discord and falsehood; an atmosphere of joy, harmony and freshness will predominate. No other environments and institutions can be found that would have no contradiction of interest and no misunderstanding among its people. No friendship between two people other than man and wife, or a parent and child can create such unity of interest with mutual understanding.

Felicity: The premise

While these words (about married life) are true and appropriate, it should be noted that, there are conditions to qualify for this undertaking. First of all a man has to be financially capable to make a living and to accommodate the family needs. Assessing the affordability (for marriage) should not, however, be made on excessive side. The possibility of taking charge of an average living condition should suffice.

Equally important is the extreme care that must be taken in choosing the mate. For selecting the mate, instead of seeking superficial and physical advantages, more attention should be paid to virtue, nobility, chastity, superior moral, health and home economic. The nominal advantages should be of secondary consideration. Looking for a woman in public gatherings and randomly, contrary to common perception, is not a proper approach because in this kind of selection, one's mind and rational thinking makes little contribution. A woman who is introduced by a wise and educated friend is likely to be more proper because unbiased and experienced friends are more credible in this enterprise.

Last but not least, there should be no negligence in making the best efforts and necessary sacrifices for proper nurturing of children. Most men who constantly complain about marriage and (dealing with) children, have neglected to observe at least one of these conditions.

Marriage: The social aspects

From the stand point of society, the act of marriage is also noteworthy. The unmarried young men for satisfying their natural desire for lust, consume their physical, mental and financial resources through illegitimate relationship and sensual acts with unscrupulous women of loose morals. Instead of forming a family, reproducing and nurturing capable and righteous children, they give away everything they have and help spread indecency and prostitution. The social losses of this behavior is much more than what can be explained in these few sentences. It is basically equivalent to a farmer who disposes his valuable seeds and the tools needed for farming into a rubbish bin, incurring all kinds of moral and economic losses for himself and others; instead of applying them towards preparation of a fertile farm and reaping the benefits of farm's fruits of his farm as well as contributing to the development of the surroundings. The unmarried youth, not only directly assists whoredom, but based on the same natural need and inclination between man and woman, indirectly leads the unmarried women astray, to prostitution, and further down, towards moral abyss.

It is obvious that the encouragement of youth to shun single life and instead to embrace the idea of forming a family would effectively help make the society, and the country healthy and strong. It reinforces the level of confidence of its people in two fronts. On the one hand, it prevents the spread of prostitution and its devastating effect, in turn, discouraging unmarried life style. On the other hand, its contribution to population increase, in turn, results in a more powerful and productive nation.

The real returns for civic duty of youth

In every society or nation, individuals must realize that structure of a humankind is socially-based and naturally they all are in need of one another; and willing or not, the morality and corruption of anyone will affect the quality of the life of another. The family and relatives' well being and good education are of great interest, and as such one does his best not to neglect the nurturing and educating of younger brothers and or sisters.

What is neglected, however, is that the good ethics and education and therefore happiness of the family and its relatives would be contingent upon morality and level of education of the families of the surroundings. This includes the public institutions such as schools, places of worship, theaters, the shopping centers and businesses which are commonly shared by all.

If the neighbors are uneducated and or debauched, it is naturally due to the contact and relationship between two neighbors one of whom will not allow the other neighbor to become educated and moralistic. In a poor tribe or country no one can claim strength and wealth. One must therefore be interested and concerned in one's own society and country because one's wealth, happiness and interest will be dependent on the others interest and happiness.

Committing to marriage and having a family prevents the spread of prostitution and its harmful damages in the society. It will help stabilize the country's population. The moral cleansing and stabilization of population of the country will gradually add to the society power and wealth, whose beneficiaries are the citizens, directly affected from such gains, both materially and morally. This action would counterbalance one's responsibility of earnings for family's living expenses and children education. Yes, marriage is one of the virtues and unchangeable laws of nature and adhering to that, both from social point of view and individual's standpoint will secure one's honor, happiness and success.

CHAPTER FIVE
Divorce according to Islam and European jurisprudence

The importance of divorce as well as its legal, social and moral aftermath are by no means less than those of marriage and it is therefore appropriate to discuss this issue at length.

On the matter of divorce, two key subjects have continually pre-occupied lawmakers attention. The first issue is whether a permission for divorce in the case of mutual consent must be granted; or, should the desire and determination of either party for divorce be sufficient. If latter should divorce be limited to a few anticipated and exceptional cases while denying many cases based on indulgence.

The second issue is whether the authority and position of man and wife on divorce should be equal, or the man alone should have the right of divorce since woman is or, presumed to be both weaker in mental power, and fainthearted; hence possibly subjected to misuse of the privilege.

The comparative applications of these two cases in Islam's Sharia and the European jurisprudence are of interest.

Divorce according to European laws

Cases for Possibility of divorce- In this scenario, one can assume that determination of man, or of either party will suffice, or both parties must give their consents, or except under the circumstances anticipated by law, divorce is not permitted.

Married couple's control of divorce- The rules of law as practiced in European countries permit general control and the equal status for the couple. Both man and wife have the same qualification and ability to apply for divorce, whether with the consent of both parties, or the desire of one of the parties, or exclusively under exceptional conditions.

A) Divorce according to the French Civil Code

According to Christianity marriage contract was considered infrangible and divorce was absolutely nonexistent. Later it became clear that continuation of some marriage contracts may become unbearable and a solution was needed for separating the man and wife who had irreconcilable differences. The solution, by lawmakers, eventually turned out to be a physical separation[1], allowing the dissatisfied couple to live separately, on a temporary basis, and in separate quarters; but retaining all relationships, rights and marriage duties, such as loyalty,..etc. Only the requirement of the husband's duty of alimony and the wife's duty of obeying and conforming were terminated, but neither the man nor the wife were able to marry and any unlawful relationships of either one was subject to prosecution. This separation had a three year period after which the couple had to resume their marriage. As of 1968, this temporary arrangement is practiced in Sweden and Rumania only; in most other west European countries it can be either temporary or permanent. In Germany, as a special case, and akin to divorce, the law allows unlimited separation upon mutual consent applicable only if one of the causes for divorce exists. Generally, in all countries where divorce is recognized after three years the party who had initiated the separation is forced to either reconcile their differences or file for formal divorce.

This unpleasant status continued until French Revolution at which time and as a natural reaction to excessive religious influence and despotic policy of Bourbons government, sweeping laws were enacted to reverse the previous laws. As an example, divorce was allowed contingent only on the determination of either party. As a result either the husband or the wife could apply for divorce for any reason at all.

Several decades later such extreme measures were moderated and when civil laws were compiled, from articles 275 onward, divorce was only authorized with both parties consent. The reasoning of lawmakers and the law was that marriage contract, just like any other contracts, required the participants consent and as such its dissolution did not require any special treatment. This law lasted until 1816 when the Bourbons returned. The over-reaction to excesses of extremists led to cancellation of most of the above-mentioned laws. The kingdom of Louis the 18th prohibited divorce, reverting to pre-revolution status which lasted until late 19th century. During this period and until 1875 many attempts were made to moderate the divorce law without much progress until the lawmakers successfully enacted a law[2] on 27th July 1884 which established divorce rules based on mutual consent, but with the following exceptions:

1$_a$) If one of the parties commits adultery the other party can file a complaint in the court and upon proving the guilt the injured party is awarded the right to divorce. Until two years after the enactment of the law (1886) there was a difference between man's and woman's being guilty of adultery. Woman would give her consent for divorce regardless of where the act was committed. Man would only give his consent for divorce if he had committed adultery in the married home where the two of them lived together. There is, however, another privilege for man which allows man the right to always prosecute his adulterous woman in criminal court, while the woman can only do so if the man has committed adultery in the home that married couple lived together[3].

2$_a$) According to article 232 if one of the parties is convicted of crime, punishable by imprisonment with hard labor or crime with lesser degree of punishment, the other party is given the right to file for divorce.

3$_a$) According to article 231 in the case of abusiveness and strong incompatibility of either party if proven to the court, the right of divorce is awarded to the injured party.

Other than the above exceptions the physical separation, as described before, is also counted as a similar exception

Processes of divorce execution- A party that is filing for divorce must appear before the magistrate at the court accompanied by the other party informing the judge the subject matter. The judge, in turn, would warn both parties of the consequences, while advising them to settle their differences. If that is not accepted he provides the divorce application to the applicant. After submission of written application both parties are invited on an appointed date and time that perhaps can facilitate an amicable settlement. If there are no resolutions the court will investigate and if the applicant's complaint is substantiated the court will rule in favor of divorce. This ruling can be appealed. The divorce particulars must be recorded in both parties personal identification documents.

Effects of divorce- Upon recording the contents of divorce, the marriage contract is quashed and each party is free to re-marry, but woman, according to article 301, must "promise" to wait nine months before re-marrying. The same article prescribes that the court must determine a payment as expense supplement to be made by the requester of divorce to the party who is divorced, based on the couple's living condition, their habits and their financial means. If the couple has a child who is minor he must be placed under the care of requester (of divorce)[4].

According to article 299 the divorced party *cannot* use the assets and other rights given to the other party, as gift during their married life or on the wedding day.

According to a law enacted on 6th February 1793, after a divorce is finalized the woman must use her maiden name. Finally as noted before, woman regains her complete legal personality which she had lost after her marriage.

B) Divorce according to other European countries jurisprudence

After the French Revolution, divorce was gradually accepted in most European countries except for Italy and Portugal where only physical separation was allowed. In Italy divorce is available to foreigners whose national laws allow divorce, meaning that there is no conflict with good morals and public sentiments. In Portugal, by contrast, divorce is prohibited and is considered inconsistent with good morals and public order[5]. Countries that have conditionally incorporated divorce in their civil laws are: Sweden, Norway, Denmark, Belgium, Spain, France (Civil Code article 299), Luxembourg (article 299), Holland (article 254), Switzerland(article 43, law enacted in 1874 and later replaced by article 137 as the approved new law in 1907 and implemented 1st January 1912) Germany (article 1564). In Austria and Russia (prior to 1917 Russian revolution) divorce was available only to certain classes of the nation members of the empire.

In some countries if a wife commits adultery or makes a bad faith attempt against her husband's life she will be denied the right to re-marry. The causes of divorce in France, Belgium and Luxembourg are almost the same except that in France, the penalty for criminal conviction must be accompanied with hard labor and demeaning to humans[6], but in Belgium and Luxembourg criminal conviction goes not include hard labor. In Belgium and Luxembourg if man commits adultery he will yield his right of divorce to his wife if and when he keeps his mistress in their married home, but in France one time relationship as adulterer is enough for the husband to relinquish his right of divorce in favor of his wife. In Portugal and Italy a husband's adultery does not always lead to physical separation unless he keeps the alien woman openly in their married home or elsewhere, or if the wife leaves her married home. In these two countries due to absence of divorce the lawmakers have added the above causes for cancellation of the marriage contract as well as physical separation. In Italy, the husband's leaving home at will, or threatening the wife, or lack of being stationary in one town without a good reason, or by constantly moving about from one town to another will be causes for separation. In Portugal if a woman is accused and prosecuted for adultery and subsequently acquitted she will be given the right for physical separation.

In Switzerland, in addition to provisions for special cases, if and when either or both spouses seek divorce and it is proven to the court that the marriage is unsustainable; then the court upon being convinced of the lack of marriage relationships and sincerity, will rule in favor of divorce. In Sweden the king has the right to grant divorce in cases such as excessive drinking and abusing of either spouses as well as mutual hatred and grudges which are some of the causes not legislated or carried out by court of law.

C) Dementedness of spouse as viewed by Germany and France

In Germany, as well as Switzerland and Sweden, an incurable mental disorder for either spouses did entitle the other spouse to the right of divorce[7]. In Sweden this was on condition that the cause or the origin of this disturbance did not result from the behavior or action of the other party. On the contrary, according to the laws of France and Belgium madness did not entitle one party the right of divorce, rather the healthy spouse had to nurse and care for the sick spouse.

The rationale of the first three countries was that an unsustainable marriage should end because in such a case the marriage was practically meaningless. In fact during this period the healthy spouse was deprived from his or her reproduction right and any addition of newborns to the family was suspended; hence denying expansion of family. On the other hand, reproduction by the mentally diseased or impaired spouse must be considered unsafe and hence should be avoided.

Generally, the reason for awarding divorce in the past two countries was that if one of the spouses is proven to be guilty that spouse has caused injury to, or has damaged the standing and honor of, the other spouse. Regarding mental disorder, this generalization fails because no fault could be attributed to the sick spouse. Furthermore, morals, humanity and sincerity of marriage prevents one from leaving the other spouse without any care.

One of the French scholars of law states: "...lawmakers of Germany, Sweden, Switzerland have given a bad lesson and example to their nations regarding individual's sacrifice because they have suggested and persuaded a sense of selfishness, comfort seeking, uncaring attitude for human feelings as well as social insensitivity ..". The reality, however, was other than this because the intent was to put an end to a fruitless and unpleasant marriage. It also prevented the reproduction of demented newborn. Besides, a spouse with the potential of being a parent of several children should not be kept in suspense with no good options. To make up for this moral deficiency, all three countries, namely, German civil law, article 1583, Swiss civil law, article 152 and Swede royal order of year 1810 compelled the spouse who was given the right to divorce to compensate the mentally ill spouse as long as the illness lasted and in proportion to his or her wealth.

In all three countries' jurisprudence a fundamental rule now exists that if the spouse who has consented to divorce is innocent, say, the wife and the other spouse, who receives the right of divorce is guilty, the husband; even if the husband has not personally requested divorce and the court has imposed that on that party; nevertheless the guilty party, the husband, is bound to provide the financial assistance to the guiltless and injured party as long as that party lives. The law in the case of the spouse with mental illness, who has been left alone, considers it to be equivalent to the innocent "giver" of divorce and the healthy spouse, who has left her, is interpreted as being the "receiver" of divorce, whose guilt is established and has caused the divorce. Therefore the receiver of divorce is compelled to pay alimony to the ill spouse.

The above overview of the European laws regarding possible causes show that the laws of west Europeans, generally have not allowed marriage to be a freely elected relationship whose contractual obligations as well as cancellation or termination be subjected to desire of either party. In fact, for the privilege of a legal marriage as opposed to illegitimate ones, certain ceremonial affairs and obligations are required. For instance, as detailed before, between the ages of eighteen to twenty-one (the legal age of maturity for woman and man) the permission for marriage is required and from the ages of twenty-one to twenty five years, consultation and consent of guardian is needed. Furthermore, to officiate the marriage both bride and bridegroom must present themselves along with others and openly declare their intention to marry. Before the marriage ceremony the matter must be advertised for public knowledge inside the municipality premises, with the notice posted on board viewable by everybody. Ten days are set aside for any objections or complaints that can be expressed by any relatives of the couple and interested party.

In a similar fashion, the mere mutual consent of the parties is insufficient for divorce. For any separation the court must investigate and rule on the merit of the request for separation. The lawmakers' intent has been, on the one hand, to preserve the marriage which is the means of uniting a man and a woman as the source for reproduction and continuity of humankind and hence families for the purpose of increasing the populous. On the other hand, the laws do not allow the dissolution of marriage under the influence of youth, derived from ignorance or sensual desire of either party or both.

In reality, the court of law should give a guilty verdict to the spouse who has tarnished the other spouse's social status and consciousness. A set of laws and a group of legislatures generally tend to support this idea; nevertheless the fact remains that an unsustainable marriage must be dissolved as soon as possible and to relieve the spouses from bearing any torments.

The followers of strict rules of marriage who are motivated by religious teachings have attempted to be mindful of the religious principles based on unbreakability of marriage contract. Another group that prescribes dissolution of marriage has freed itself from any restrictions; subsequently, experiencing increased demand for legal assistance which is needed by divorce seekers.

To conclude, the first group has considered the basic and the important benefits to the society, namely, the strength of marriage contract and the difficulty in breaking it. The second group has taken the position of accommodating individual's comfort and restfulness, namely, the possibility of separation in case of an incompatible marriage. At any event, as mentioned before, the authority and ability of a couple to apply for divorce would be equal and alike. The laws reflect the influence and growth of women's social rights with no particular privileges being reserved for man.

D) Divorce according to Islam

Islam treats the marriage affair and its **dissolution** with extreme care and thought because it is the effective driver of social structure of a family and therefore society; specifically it is considered a ceremonial occasion. Islam provides every facility and convenience for the purpose of promoting and propagating marriage events and encourages marriage ceremonies. From the viewpoint of protocols the presence of two witnesses would be, recommended by religious teachings, but required by social customs for the execution of the contract document.

An item-by-item description of all the faults of both parties is presented to officiating person that could be a cause for cancellation of marriage contract by each party.

Both marriage contract and its dissolution, divorce testimony, require specific guidelines that the parties must follow. To discourage divorce, on the other hand, certain conditions are set forth making its execution fraught with various difficulties.

In short, Islam's Sharia, considers, above all, the social aspect of marriage as the strength of the foundation of society's structure, and to establish such claim it lays out four principles.

First, it does not allow termination or breaking of the marriage contract contrary to all other contracts. Second, it generally assumes that man's physical, mental and moral structure is stronger, more active and more rational than woman's. Accordingly, it has trusted the authority for divorce to the man. This preserves the families' status intact and unaffected by women's emotional upheaval or anger as well as sentimental feelings and tenderness. Third, to prevent the spread of an endemic divorce it has enacted a series of directives and impediments to slow or stop those divorce cases that have no or little rational or understandable basis. Fourth, to balance the man's obstinacy regarding divorce, both positively and negatively, it provides certain rules protecting the rights of the couple, as described below. The protection addresses some key issues as to whether an innocent woman is being divorced unilaterally and unfairly, or a wife is treated unfairly by the man who refuses to divorce her, which she desperately wants.

d$_1$) Elements of divorce

Divorce according to Islam's jurisprudence contains four major components. These elements are then applied to the various types of divorce.

i) The giver of divorce

The divorce giver must be of a sound mind, be of legal age and have the intent and control of his faculties. If the person is deficient of any of these conditions the divorce is void. Accordingly, divorcing the person who, suffers periodic or temporary relapse, or is about to go mad, or is permanently mad, or is in the state of sleep, or is reluctant to receive divorce an, or is experiencing financial difficulties will not take effect. The reluctance of the receiver of divorce is confirmed if threat(by the giver of divorce) is used in the event that the order is not carried out which may be contingent upon the person's ability to do. The nature of the threat may directly affect the person in question or another person, that is, a close relative of child.

ii) The receiver of divorce

The divorce receiver must meet four conditions. First, a permanent marriage which rules out that of slave in which case freeing of slave replaces divorce; this by itself is quite significant in the 7th century. Second, she must be free from menstrual discharge and child birth[8]. Third, divorce must take place when the woman is cleansed such that no intercourse between the husband and the wife has taken place. Fourth, the wife being divorced must be specified; therefore if a man has two wives and divorces one without specifying, the divorce is invalid. The reason is that the in the marriage contract which is now the subject of dissolution specifies the name of the wife that must match that of the person who is being divorced.

iii) Directives for divorce

The directives must be clear and definitive so that there will be no opportunity for doubt about the intent of the divorce giver of what is clearly explained. For example it should not be a mere informative text, but a narrative.

iv) Witnesses
The Prophet has clearly expressed his disapproval of divorce :

"No allowable act is more unbecoming than divorce"; or, "I hate divorce more than anything" .

Divorce, according to Islam, is indeed an unpleasant and indecent act. The happening of divorce must accordingly be discouraged, making it contingent upon difficult conditions and special requirements in order to control its application process. That is the reason behind the opinion of Shia jurists regarding the presence of two witnesses during the divorce execution. Justice in divorce, according to some jurists is considered real justice; therefore the mere "appearing just to be moral" is insufficient. Conversely, civil jurist do not consider the presence of witnesses as a "condition", although they do consider it necessary for marriage contract.

d_2) Types of divorce
Three types of divorce are foreseen according to Islam's Sharia.

i) Ba'en divorce where the husband is forbidden to reclaim, or return to his ex-wife; after being divorced. (rojoo'). The women in this category include: a divorcee who has not cohabited with her husband (Gheire -e-Madkhouleh), an under-aged divorcee and the incompetent divorcee.

ii) Mokhtala' and Mobarat divorce: In the event that the divorcee had already endowed (Bazl) to her husband and has not reclaimed it, her ex-husband is forbidden to return to her after divorce is granted; otherwise, the husband has the right to reclaim her within the prescribed period (Eddeh). Finally, if the wife is divorced three times and the husband has performed the act of reclaiming his ex-wife twice between each divorce, then the third time divorce is interpreted as Ba'en, meaning he is barred from remarrying her.

iii) *Raj'i* (rajee) divorce is a type of divorce other than the above types. It literally means revocable divorce. The husband has the right of return to the divorced wife within the specified period and regardless of whether he has applied his right or not the divorce remains valid and revocable.

Iiia) A variation to revocable divorce is *Eddeh* divorce: This type of divorce occurs when a woman has been divorced in the form of *Raj'i*, the husband has returned to her within *Eddeh* and after cohabiting, he has divorces her again. In this case it is possible that the husband for the second time within *Eddeh* remarry her, that is reclaimed ex-wife, but if he divorces her for the third time, whether cohabiting or not, he can no longer repeat the act of reclaiming his ex-wife or to marry her based on new marriage contract.

In such event(after the third divorce) he is no longer allowed to marry this woman. Only if the divorcee is re-married to another man(*Mohallel*), literally meaning the facilitator, and later divorced by him (the facilitator), would she, as a "free" woman, be able to re-marry anyone, including her original husband. If this process is repeated (nine times divorced and six times re-married to the same man) the couple will be permanently denied to be married to each other.

There is a possible scenario that a man divorces his wife and after the prescribed period has elapsed, remarry her under new contract marriage. The man is now allowed to divorce her and after the prescribed period has elapsed again to re-marry her under new marriage contract and divorce her once more, that is three times divorcing. After the third divorce, however, he cannot re-marry her under a new marriage contract unless she re-marries a facilitator. It should be noted that prior cohabiting with either her husband or the facilitator is not permitted.

The facilitator must be of legal age and had cohabited with the woman prior to possible divorce. Confirmation of this procedure requires that cohabitation to have taken place right after the marriage ceremony upon the execution of marriage contract.

d₃) Explanation of term: Eddeh

Eddeh in general refers to a specified prescribed period. For example it refers to a period during which the divorcee abstains from re-marrying. Apparently the intent is to protect woman's womb from other than family root. Accordingly, a divorcee who has *not* cohabited with her husband does not have any *Eddeh* as obligation. Also, if the separation results in termination of marriage contract the same applies. *Eddeh* is the end of three cleansing of woman; even if the cleansing is one instant before the occurrence of woman's menstrual begins, that instant is considered "a cleansing".

Those women who are in the right age bracket of reproduction, but due to physical conditions do not have the monthly discharge, the end of 3-month window will be sufficient. With regards to women who have not cohabited with their husband and the incompetent or retard one (*ya'seh*) the opinion of Shia jurists vary. Most believe that since the reference point and criterion for *Eddeh* is to prevent mixed blood relation, there is no need to keep track of *Eddeh* regarding this class of women.

If the divorcee after the expiration of a specified period is suspected of being pregnant, i.e. exhibiting negligible signs to that effect, she can re-marry and if after her marriage she actually becomes pregnant the marriage contract is not voided. However she should not have married if the specified *period* had not expired. If she had married after the expiration date and her pregnancy had later become a reality that marriage would be null and void because she had definitely been pregnant during the time that specified prescribed period was in-play. The specified prescribed *period* of a pregnant woman cannot be aborted other than giving birth. In the case of a deceased husband, specified prescribed period is four months and ten days from his date of death, but if the wife was pregnant at the time the longest date is to be observed. This means that

212

if after four months and ten days the woman is still pregnant she must wait until the baby is born before re-marrying.

In the case of divorce type of *Raj'i*, the man is obliged to keep the woman at his home for the duration of her specified prescribed period. The woman must not leave home without the man's consent except for the essential needs. The woman's expenses during the period of specified prescribed period, including food and clothes is the responsibility of the man. In case of irrevocable divorce the woman is free to go anywhere and the man has no responsibility to pay for her expenses except if and when she is pregnant; whereupon in case of irrevocable divorce the expenses will be the man's responsibility. In the event of death of the husband and during the period of specified prescribed period the divorced woman claims no share of her husband's inheritance[9]. If the woman is pregnant at the time some believe woman's necessary expenses should be paid from the assets that the fetus will inherit.

Mokhala', Khal' and *Mobarat* divorce: These are variations of divorce type of irrevocable. The particularity of these types of divorce is that woman in return for getting a divorce without the husband's right of Rojoo', would give some asset of her own to the husband and during the period of *Eddeh*, as long as she has not revoked her largess, the husband does not have the right of *Rojoo'*. Type *Khal'* divorce is based on the assumption that the wife is unhappy and hates her husband and the assets that she has given to the husband may exceed her dowry. Type *Mobarat divorce* is based on the assumption that both husband and wife are unhappy with each other and the wife's gift does not exceed her dowry.

Regarding the irreconcilable differences between man and wife, a gathering of relatives (and in absence of that, close friends) should investigate the couple's differences and attempt to reconcile the parties, but this gathering is not authorized to recommend divorce without the husband's consent. Also, unless the wife consents her right of exchanging gifts for divorce will remain valid.

d₄) Temporary separation, Ila'
In conclusion of describing various types of divorce it is appropriate to take notice of a provision in Islam's Sharia known as temporary separation that may be a prelude to divorce. The term *Ila'* refers to a temporary non-cohabitation based on the husband's swearing that he would absolutely abstain from approaching his wife for the period of more than four months. After this period, the couple will either agree to divorce or to reconcile and resume their married life. If latter, an atonement for swearing is due whether or not the cohabitation has taken place during that period.

E) Christians criticism
In their critical review of Islam's Sharia, Christians raise three important issues, related to the subject of divorce, that need to be addressed. First, the early learned Christians were of the opinion that divorce was an abominable and unpleasant act and since it did not exist in Christianity it must also be excluded from consideration by other religious laws and therefore Islam's law allowing divorce is subject to criticism. Second, since no special cases for possibility of divorce are even considered and man's determination alone matters, therefore divorce is propagated and the foundation of families is threatened to destruction and extinction. Third, since the determination of divorce is given to man in many cases the woman, negatively or positively, is left oppressed and hopeless. Many women want to be freed from their husbands who would refuse to comply with their wishes; and conversely, many faultless women are divorced because of their ungrateful husbands' false desires and excessive indulgences. These are serious issues which deserve to be analyzed based on facts, real circumstances and without any bias.

Permission for divorce

Voltaire, the French writer and scholar says: "marriage and divorce are born together, only marriage is a few weeks older; the couple have an argument in the second week, a fight in the third week and are divorced in the fourth week". This satire is an allusion to the necessity of divorce existence in a civil society. It is surprising that since divorce does not exist in Christianity, Islam should be faulted for not doing so.

That divorce has not been foreseen in Christianity is not surprising because marriage, which is also of the primitive desire of mankind and a necessary means of creation, has also not been promoted or recommended in Early Christianity; in fact the solitary life was practiced by monks and celibacy became standard in the Middle Ages. Christianity, is not able to relieve the civil related and political needs of societies on matters of social customs, habits and rules; it is a spiritual way not unlike gnosticism. It cannot even be interpreted as principles of morality in social context of society's morals. Indeed, attention should be given only from the viewpoint of individual's morals and guiding of people as individuals.

Islam's Sharia, on the other hand, is a social religion which for fourteen centuries has been able to guide and lead hundreds of millions of Muslims socially, politically and morally. Before Christ, religious laws such as Hammurabi and Hebrew had prescribed divorce. Civil laws of Christian nations also, in accordance with societies' needs and necessities, and over the church's objection, have accepted divorce as described in previous section. Islam's Sharia, which is in harmony with every aspect of social laws and traditions as related to creation, was obliged not to prohibit divorce. This bitter medicine is, under special circumstances, an effective remedy for salvation of a couple. For those who have been unable to reconcile their differences for an extended period, divorce is the best remedy considering the circumstances. Study of the rules of divorce and prevailing conditions according to Islam shows that it is prescribed in the most expeditious manner and by the best method. The Prophet has said:

"Divorce is viewed by God as the most spiteful of what is ceremonially clean, *halals*"; meaning the least lawful.

Before Islam, a vicious cycle of divorcing followed by re-marrying the divorced wife was prevalent and boundless in Arabia. Islam limited this practice to only two times. The third time, if requested by the man, the matter had to be investigated by a family gathering of both the husband and the wife to recommend solutions prior to divorce. The families of the couple would recommend that the husband should either avoid divorcing his wife on compassionate ground and good behavior, or letting her go as a gesture of fairness and good work for ever.

As explained before, the third time that a husband divorces his wife he is barred from remarrying here. There is, however a possibility that the wife marries someone else and later her new husband divorces her. This opens an opportunity for her ex husband to again reunite with her. The man who has made this possible is known as facilitator(*Mohallel*); a special case in Islam's rules of divorce. Some leaders of Christians have criticized Sharia by portraying a man being forced to surrender his ex-wife to a stranger in order to be able to re-claim her as his lawful wife. To clarify this, they should first study Islam's view and its objective towards discouraging divorce and make their judgement accordingly.

There are two key issues here that are under consideration. Issue one is the "best effort" made to prevent divorce; as demanded by both parties who are slaves to carnal desire and indulgence as well as bouts of sadness or anger. Ideally the best effort to discourage the couple to divorce would be a persuasive argument that would convince the couple that divorce destroys the foundation of their family and ultimately break up their home a place for joint nurturing of their children. Sadly a stronger motivation is needed to dissuade the couple from separation.

Islam has imposed several difficult tasks and conditions to discourage the possibility of occurrence of divorce compiled as Islam's principle of divorce which is loaded with several obstacles. Even if divorce is finalized there is yet another provision for an extended "prescribed waiting period " as the last resort of necessity. This provision allows a compulsory cooling off period. The rationale for this provision is that if the decision to divorce had initially no logic or reasonable cause and was driven by anger and instant unhappiness after several days of peace and tranquility the husband per chance is ready to reconcile and the couple will jointly resume, their most important task of nurturing their children.

The second issue viewed by Islam is the personality and prestige of the wife in every respect that must be protected. Islam aimed for reciprocity between the husband and the wife, after divorce leads to possible reconciliation. The couple must equally enjoy the same treatment from each other. To understand this almost unattainable goal for woman, consider a playing field of polo where a player riding a horse strikes a ball to the direction of another rider and so on. This game was a playful act manifesting man's sensual representation in Arabia before Islam. The least valued tool in this game was the playing ball which were considered worthless as compared to the horses and men's garments. This was an indication as how men valued their women in Arabia (and most of the world for that matter) in the 7th century. In this simple example one can imagine that equal treatment of the husband and the wife with such unequal statures was non existent. A man who divorced his wife could re-claim her as many time as he desired and at anytime. Islam limited this unbounded reclamation of his ex-wife. Twice it was allowed, but divorcing for the third time would break the cycle of re-claiming the ex-wife. It would then be necessary that woman be freed from the yoke of her ex-husband; and she would be free to marry any man she would choose.As such, divorce though spiteful and destructive is therefore allowed by Islam.

The new husband had to be a man of legal age and unrelated to the ex-husband of the woman. Furthermore, the woman and the new husband by executing a marriage contract, followed by marriage ceremony, would resume a married life. The new marriage included all the formalities such as a new contract, new protocols, new dowry and the woman's consent.

Islam took into account the probability that, no matter how small and remote, the newly wedded couple may divorce at some point. If such an event took place and if subsequently the first ex-husband and his newly divorced ex-wife were both interested in re-uniting, they could then re-marry anew. Under such scenario the just- divorced man has been instrumental to make the original couple to reunite; therefore he is called the facilitator. This process may itself be repeated, with almost zero probability, but the third time the cycle ends and even the second time facilitator will not work, i.e., the maximum number of times that a man can re-marry his ex-wife is nine times.

The facilitator therefore serves as an effective deterrent *because* the third time a man divorces his wife would be the last chance for his reclaiming his ex-wife. If his rationale for divorce is valid, the resulting divorce will lead to peace of mind for both parties. If the desire to divorce is, however, based on artificial unhappiness or indulgence this will be his last chance to avert a permanent rupture with his wife. He should particularly be concerned with the prospect of another man possessing his ex-wife and a sense of jealousy and bias could force him to re-think his decision hence not to divorce. Islam by introducing the idea of facilitator, has indirectly condemned both the act of divorce and the person who would take advantage of misery of one man for his personal pleasure. The Prophet has said:

"Should I not inform you of a borrowed goat?

"It is the facilitator. God's curse on him and on the person who would legitimize his wife in this way".

Spread of divorce
The rules of divorce contain general cases that justify the possibilities of divorce, and particular circumstances when divorce is likely to occur.

It is true that according to Islam's Sharia the man is authorized to divorce his wife; this act may be due to man's spontaneous anger or uncontrolled emotions or any other circumstances which, by itself, can result in an uncontrollable wide spread propagation of many divorce cases. The question is why Islam religion empowered a man with such power and what safeguards, if any, were provided to offset this deficiency.

Legal Status of divorce before Islam
It is a historical fact that man has exclusively inherited such rights from the ancient times, well before the coming of Islam and was applying those rights with extreme cruelty and harshness, a glimpse of which could be traced to Judaism, Hammurabi laws as well as the laws of Brahma, and Buddhism in China and India.

In general Islam considers the man a creature struggling for survival; physically stronger, more active and more resolute than woman. For these reasons it has vested the responsibility of providing the sustenance for his family's livelihood with him; and the burden of hardship to accomplish this task rests on his shoulders alone. Furthermore, Islam has considered the woman's emotions influenced by her sensitivities and irrational affections which may be detrimental to the stability and durability of her family and hence not the decider in seeking divorce.

With the above in mind, Islam could not have taken away the ancient rights (no matter how unjust) in a short time and present them to the woman. The woman was barely prepared to take charge of her just-acquired freedom and independence and only in incremental steps. For her to impose her will in such critical social matter would have created chaos. Accordingly the power of permitting divorce was given to the man.

Islam's fundamental changes

Accordingly Islam adopted two effective approaches to harness the rights of a man as the giver of divorce. One, the path of education to guide the man to morality by way of religious teachings and strengthening his faith in God and moral laws; another to create obstacles and various extraordinary conditions and complexity to discourage divorce. With respect to the path of education Islam trained a Muslim man in such a way that under no circumstances a believing man who abides by religious rules will oppress his wife. He will not conduct himself as being indulgent, lustful and insensitive person by divorcing a guiltless wife. The Prophet preached the importance of mutually good behavior of a couple on many occasions which were both significant and historical. For example, during his last pilgrimage he addressed one hundred and twenty-thousands Muslims, when he reminded men of good behavior towards women; and again, at the most sensitive juncture of his life, just before passing. His will was the reminder, again, that good behavior towards woman is placed as one of the conditions of complete faith in God. In Early Islam, observing the rights of the woman and her fair treatment were commonplace; and Islam's leaders actively promoted this practice to a degree that almost any ill treatment of a woman and her subsequent divorce were considered inappropriate. Men, committing such unacceptable acts were harshly criticized and were even considered social outcasts.

As for inventing restrictions, the qualitative aspect of divorce in Islam dictates that before the couple's disagreements and discords lead to divorce and break-up of the family, serious efforts for reconciling their differences must be made. If reconciliation is not successful then divorce must only be executed in the office of magistrate in presence of two just witnesses, pronouncing a special directive. The giver of divorce must be alert, of legal age, having the intent and the authority.

The receiver of divorce must be cleansed from menstrual discharge and child birth and cleansed from other than sexual intercourse (i.e., physically clean). The witnesses must be male and truly just. Divorce directive must be unambiguous and unconditional. In each session only one divorce case is executed. During the prescribed waiting period, the wife has to live in her husband's quarters. If the cause of divorce is temporary depression, after several days the husband's mental condition may improve and his anger may subside. The slightest sign indicating an inclination of the husband towards his wife would lead to re-uniting of the couple.

If the cause of divorce involves more serious issues and the couple are just not able or willing to get along, then the continuation of this marriage will result in a soul-exhausting torture and divorce may be the best option for the parties. It is notable that, since the wife (while married) generally does not claim her dowry out of sincerity and unity of interest, the man must pay her dowry after divorce is finalized.

In conclusion, because of many restrictions and other ceremonial chores, as well as creating opportunities for re-uniting of the couple, in many cases, divorce could be prevented from happening.

Some statistics on divorce

Tolstoy, the Russian writer is quoted to have said that the real reason for widespread divorce in some societies, is the frivolousness of women thinking that they are capable of doing anything men can do. An unconfirmed research was compiled by(presumably Lintier), an English philosopher who lived in several Muslim countries for a period of fifty-four years starting from 1848. The paper suggests that fewer divorces occurred in that period(among Muslims) than among other communities where the research was conducted. Separately, some published statistics[10] indicate that in the US some 148,554 divorces took place in 1923 a significant increase from 70,000 in 1922 and 50,000 in the entire period of 1917-21. Another publication[11] in an article titled *American Tragedy* estimates divorce in the US ; "According to new statistics, in the US, in every sixty marriages ten of them result in divorces".

The above data underlines the fundamental issues of today's society's morals. In a typical consumer oriented society of today women have been led to believe that the excessive spending and superficial changes in the style of living, that would ultimately contribute to more consumption, is somehow a manifestation of their freedom. This leads to the belief that for a woman to acquire such privileges she must become more demanding and hence more "desirable" to men. Women's focus is then to have a husband to accommodate their comfort and satisfy their urge to consume more. Both men and women in such society have equal shared responsibility for spreading divorce because neither of them has understood the spirit and meaning of marriage.

Today's husband frees himself from tending to his family by, working long hours and as much as he can bear, indulging himself with sensuality. He would take pride in showing off his wife to others in social gatherings, restaurants and night clubs. His wife is of course free to do whatever she desires. Yet, the man cannot satisfy all that his wife desires. In short, the woman, except for her husband's specialized skill, considers him unworthy and as a result not fit to manage her and naturally does not look at him kindly. At this juncture, the couple is engulfed in over-consumption and the associated social habits and divorce becomes the real option left for them.

One is amazed of the shallow discussions between the husband and his wife, which is not at all related to expanding their minds. They only speak about trivial issues and pay no attention to the meaning of marriage being a pact between the couple for their mutual benefits on all aspects of life, whether natural, economics, moral or spiritual. Most of the dissatisfactions stem from women's sexual expectations. These "freed" women, perhaps all around the world, are captive to sexual inclination, or at least they pretend to be. This matter is of course more pronounced in

222

consumer-oriented societies than poorer nations because their people are not yet fully "developed". Even if a woman is not particularly active in this respect her co-workers and friends would encourage her for wanting more. They are also encouraged by media toward these irrational feelings.

Women consider weddings as a trade and a man is measured according to his financial means. This leads the man to evaluate and assess such a woman, as if she is a merchandise, according to her physical attraction. Naturally, a woman who is expert in home economic, but not the most attractive is less valuable; a woman wants to get ahead of her competitors. If a man is faced with distress or unenviable circumstance, even temporarily, the woman discounts him.

There are of course women who are less "modern". For them beauty and disposition are not as precious as for others; for them the maturity and readiness is the prime objective. At any event, there should be little doubt that in countries where woman's role in initiating divorce is significant the rate of divorce is higher than other parts of the world. French courts in 1890 ruled on 9,785 cases of divorce from which 7,000 were petitioned by women[12].

Status of woman regarding divorce
There are two different situations that can be assumed, where encroachment to the woman may occur.

The first case occurs when a physically fit, healthy, virtuous and moral woman has spent her youth, her only asset, with her husband and now at an old age of debility her husband, blinded by self- indulgence and gratification, wants to divorce her. The remedy for this unjust and ungratefulness, as discussed in previous chapters, is correct social education and man's commitment to religious and moral regulations and rules. Even the best civil laws cannot guarantee individual rights and prevent encroachment from one to another when they apply to those people who lack proper moral education. Therefore with progressive

teachings of morality which Islam's Sharia has bestowed to its followers there shall be no concern about such unfairness. In the event that
a man is unencumbered by human feeling and is uncommitted to his
religious duties and morals, feeling that such wrongful conduct to his
wife was admissible then it will be best for the wife to be released and
freed from such living condition that is in fact a torture and consuming
her soul.

There may be other laws that would limit divorce to special cases and
let the woman's determination play a part, still the husband who lacks
morals can mistreat his wife and force her to ask for divorce. It can then
be stated that whether woman is having a say in divorce or not it matters
little because it is a rarity that a man after years of companionship with
his wife and children and without any guilt from his wife would decide
to divorce her just because of self-indulgence.

The second topic is more of practical usage and therefore of interest.
It is the case of a woman who is harassed by an unsuitable husband,
wanting to rid herself from his diabolical and torturous life by separation. Since the authority for getting divorce rests wit the husband
she would be unable to succeed in obtaining divorce. To rectify this
situation, first, the woman is allowed to secure her right of divorce
for special cases such as bad behavior at the time of signing her marriage contract. Second, woman can petition the local court for permission to divorce by proving that her living with the husband will
endanger her life, her financial position or her prestige. Additionally
she can petition the governor or the town official if the husband
refuses to give back her dowry or if she is not able to force him to
pay for it.

In general, Islam's Sharia has declared in all of its rulings and mandates,
including exceptional cases, that protection of the rights of individuals
is ensured and that no one should suffer from hardship or lack the necessities (osr -o- haraj). It is, therefore, categorically stated:

"placing anyone under distress or making one indigent is not allowed in Islam".

Islam, therefore, has not created any conditions that would otherwise require "relief from the suffering". According to this principle any woman who truly suffers from hardship by living with her husband may petition local authorities for getting a divorce.

In summary, Islam's Sharia, according to above mentioned introduction, compels the husband as the sole provider of alimony. The woman, on the other hand, must not at all share the burden of this heavy load. In addition, all the entire woman's assets are hers and under her control alone. Furthermore, the husband must pay a specified cash for wife's dowry, known as *Mehrieh*. In return for these benefits, the authority for divorce is given to the husband. Alimony for their children, if and when divorced, as well as the duty of taking care of the children including their education will be the father's responsibility. On the other hand for a woman who cannot continue her marriage because of her husband's bad behavior, it is possible in several ways to divorce her husband, with or without giving-up her dowry. All three cases mentioned in the French civil laws for possible causes of divorce are also contained in Sharia under "relief-from-suffering"(osr -o- haraj[13]).

Islam makes the husband responsible for everyday subsistence including all the associated hardship based on his being stronger of the pair and in return expects sincerity and loyalty (from the wife). As for divorce, in return for carrying the burden of difficulties in meeting his obligations the man is allowed to divorce his wife with whom he no longer wants to, or cannot live. The woman is also given the right to petition a court (or local authority), if her husband refuses to grant her permission for divorce, from a man with whom she has irreconcilable differences[14].

It is not at all fair to perceive that Islam's teachings on the matter of marriage and divorce and in light of the explanations presented, have not properly observed the Muslim women's rights and that women could be possibly subjected to encroachment or oppression. On the contrary, all possible efforts are made to combine the two key goals together, namely, strengthening the foundation of the family and the indisputable rights of women in every respect.

This book was first published in 1940 and yet, it does correspond with Iranian Family Protection Laws enacted in 1967 because of insertion of provisions for divorce court that correspond with principle of *Osr-o-haraj*. The cases rejected by the divorce are those that have no moral or family-related basis and are mostly caused by either or both parties' indulgence or temporary feelings, rushing to divorce only to remarry right after. In such cases the moral teachings of Islam will never allow divorce. The only deficiency that appears in this Family Protection Laws is the finality of the court ruling on divorce; rather than allowing an appropriate and immediate appeal to rectify any errors that may have occurred.

CHAPTER SIX

Inheritance according to Islam and European jurisprudence

The issue of inheritance and the relevant and various laws applied to daughters, sisters and wives can be studied from three different points of view.

- Authority of a married woman to draw a will with respect to her own assets and Estate

- The rights of the wife with respect to estates of her husband and son or, in other words, inheritance of spouse and mother.

- The rights of the daughter with respect to her father's inheritance and basic standard for her share among the inheritors.

Before describing each category in details, there are two important and basic principles which are prerequisites for all the laws and rules implemented throughout the world. The division of inheritance is distributed on the basis of either blood relation, or attachment, compassion and heart-felt closeness of the deceased to the heir.

First Principle

Blood-relation, also referred to as consanguine, allows the nearest blood-relation to the deceased become the sole inheritor and denies the rest. This means the deceased is also denied the right to transfer his wealth to anyone he desires, *succession abintestat*. This nearly universal principle, observed by Islam and the compiled civil laws, prescribes that only the children who possess father's blood as well as the parents of the deceased who share his blood are entitled to his inheritance.

This principle was applied by the Germans to the utmost before it moderated under the influence of the Romans. The laws and customs of the Germans focus on two issues resulted from this principle. The first issue is to deny any distribution bequeathed by drawing a will. The strict adherence to rules, was enforced according to the laws, as viewed by the lawmakers, applied to distribution of inheritance. The second issue is that by law no one is entitled to any shares of the inheritance except the blood-relations. As a result the deceased's wife, although the closest to him with respect to association and affection, would be completely denied any shares of inheritance because she does not possess his blood. Further, her husband was not allowed to bequeath her any portion of the inheritance by drawing a will as an expression of his heart-felt appreciation.

The Germanic culture and social habits due to the influence of the Romans as well as the sign of respect for the deceased, accepted the principle of bequeathing allowing the deceased will as an accepted way of distribution. In the other parts of Europe such as France, Belgium and Holland, however, the original rules and practiced habits were only partially modified. For example bequeathing through a will was not allowed if the deceased bequeathed his entire inheritance. In fact it is almost universal that only a prescribed amount of the inheritance could be transferred. The bequeather, of course could however donate all of his wealth to anyone while he is alive.

Second Principle

This principle states that the wish and the desire of the deceased and his heart-felt affection with respect to others must be fully respected. Since he is the owner of his wealth and he alone is in control of his assets, while alive, he has a right to prepare a testimony that his wealth be distributed as he wishes after his death. This principle, previously observed in the general Roman law is known as *Succssion testametaire* under the French laws; it is based on a mutual affection between the deceased and his inheritors. In this respect for the first time the spouses inherit from one another even though the heirs that are blood related exist in the family. The inheritance based on this principle is more prevalent in South America, Italy, Spain, Portugal, Austria and Germany than elsewhere; in England, this practice is only applicable to liquid assets.

In order to search for the historical basis and source of origin of the above two principles, one must refer to the thinking process of various nations as well as their appreciation of ownership.

A) In a span of nearly twenty five centuries the distribution of inheritance has followed the blood-relation principle and the deceased has not been allowed to bequeath anything to anyone. In a distant past the family members had no rights of ownership according to one interpretation, and every thing in the family officially belonged to the head of a family. In fact, the entire wealth of the family was not exclusively father's; it really, and practically, belonged to all and each family members. Since the family male members owned nothing and at the same time they inherited everything, they had no right as individual to give anything away in the form of testimony. Since the assets did not exclusively belong to father but collectively belonged to all the family; as a result the father was unable to draw a will.

Accordingly the law only recognized collective ownership and considered the wealth of a family as common asset for the family members; hence establishing distribution of the wealth in accordance with blood-relation principle(subsequently nearness relation between the father and the inheritors).

The French older version of law, written prior to Napoleonic Civil Code, for the purpose of distributing inheritance considered the type and nature of the wealth. The inheritance of the deceased comprised the *grand* grade wealth and the good, but *lower* grade wealth; each having different ruling. For the grand wealth two principles were followed. First, daughters were absolutely denied any part of this type of heritage. Second, the main portion of the wealth was allocated to the eldest son. The reason for denying the female member of family any inheritance was this perception that once the female member is married to someone outside the family her father's wealth will eventually transfer to an outsider.

The rationale for blood-relation distribution originated from the concept of collective ownership and the tribal-like living environment. Accordingly, the family's heritage had to remain intact within the family with a centralized authority controlled by family's father as the sole owner. In addition to this, during the Middle Ages the tribal ruling was the norm and it was customary for the bosses to keep adequate number of fighters selected from commoners within their surrounding area.

The *grand* assets were relevant to the family's aristocracy and hence a necessary reminder in deference to the fighters.

It is evident that grand assets were reserved for individuals whose existence would serve a purpose for the boss; that is why daughters and young sons were excluded from this type of assets. Regarding the *ordinary* assets; the intent was to protect the assets from being transferred outside the family. These assets were of two types; *inherited* and *acquired*.

The inherited wealth from father side or mother side would have to be retained in the deceased family, but those acquired by the deceased in his lifetime would be equally distributed among the children.

B) The concept of ownership in today's legals system, of advanced nations, is recognized as personal and individual's in contrast to collective. The Roman laws notwithstanding, one may think that the concept of inheritance based on individual ownership, and incorporated in civil laws of many nations, is very new with little background. That is not so. The origin of ownership goes back to family that was not necessarily modeled after tribal families.

Today, based on the recognized individual's and personal ownership everyone can draw all kinds of will with respect to what one owns, but still in most laws the remnants of collective ownership manifested as "family ownership" retain some degree of influence.

C) It is for this reason that in accordance with Islam's Sharia and many European countries' laws, such as those of France, Holland and Belgium a testimony which gives away more than a third of the inheritance is not binding without the expressed and a signed consent of the inheritors. After all there has to be something left of the family assets for its members. The above topics may be summed up as follows:

1. The laws of those countries that believed in collective ownership and believed that father's assets belonged to all family members, have not allowed the transfer of (family) heritage by issuing a testimony, or will. Furthermore because the criterion for distribution of inheritance was only applied to the "nearness" with the deceased with no personal attachment and affection, so their rules never allowed any shares for spouses, due to lack of blood-relationship, since each belonged to different family. Daughters were also excluded because of their eventual moving to another family quarters.

2. The laws of those nations for whom ownership was the right of an individual and a personal matter, equally take into consideration the principle of blood-sameness as well as observing the family nearness. The laws accept the prepared written will that reflects a heart-felt appreciation of the deceased expressed to one or more individuals.

Inheritance distribution in practice
In the case of individual ownership since the nominal, official and real owner of inheritance is recognized as the person who has deceased, as a general principle, the laws give bequeather the right to manage the assets in any way the person wishes. With respect to blood-sameness, attempts are made to collate the legal regulations with heart-felt feelings of the deceased in the best possible way. Although the law has prioritized the first line of children over every inheritor in the classification of the inheritors it also considers relatives nearness and the heart-felt affection of the deceased as "recommended and secured". This is because of the assumption that humankind loves his immediate children more than anyone. Similarly, the amount of affection, in proportion to nearness, is lessened, as the nearness stretches farther away and hence weaker. As such, the blood-relation and the assumed will of the deceased are both observed.

Now if someone, despite such inference and general assumption, happens to have affection for a stranger(outside the family) more than his relations he can secure his intent by drawing a will. The testimony will also be applicable for avoiding any noticeable clashes between the principle of blood-sameness and the deceased determination hence no one is being forced to bequeath his enemy(even if that happens to be his child) against his wishes.

Provisions are made by most lawmakers denying the heir from his legal share of inheritance if the death of bequeather is committed by him, either as attempted murder or homicide, direct or indirect , or the heir has knowingly concealed or withheld such information or has accused the bequeather of a crime which is later proven to be unfounded. This shows that the interest of the deceased is fully protected and observed by the laws, whether it is stated clearly or indirectly based on some assumptions.

The laws will prevent interference and imposition of individuals' intent when, under special circumstances, an exception to distribution of inheritance is made for protection of the family or community. As an example, although in principle the bequeather is empowered to do whatever he wishes with his wealth; nevertheless the law prevents the minors, those who have declared bankruptcy as well as the insane people to do anything with their assets. Furthermore, the French Civil Code until 1938, prohibited married woman to do financial transaction without the husband's permission. In these cases not only the welfare of society justified preventing certain individuals from having control over their assets, but such safeguards justified to secure the interest of the very same individuals.

In a similar manner, the inheritance laws have made the assumption that usually the heart-felt intents of the deceased should correspond to the general laws of "the creation". This means that the deceased heart-felt affection for individuals is appropriate and in proper proportion to that of the well as their blood-relations and near-relations. As such the manner in which the laws have classified, the intent of the deceased takes the interest of the inheritors in terms of shares of the inheritance into account.

As previously mentioned if someone decides, in contrast to the general rule or exceptional, prefers a distant-relative over a near-relative he can draw a will and bequeath that person with a portion of his wealth. This is contingent upon full protection of the rights of legal inheritors and as long as the will does not clash with the welfare of society. The freedom of the deceased to do so must not exceed to the point of damaging the welfare of the society and public orders.

It is interesting that both Islam's Sharia and the French Civil Code dis-allow the prepared will to exceed one third of total assets. Other laws, more or less follow a similar limitation.

Highlights

a) Presently individual ownership has replaced collective ownership and accordingly distribution of inheritance is allowed to be handled through a simple will.

b) The law permitting the deceased to apply his full authority and bequeath all of his inheritance to outsiders and deny any portions to legal inheritors, against the laws of nature, is rarely used.

c) For the type of legal inheritance which respects the deceased inclina-tion and heart-felt feeling for his wife and companion who enjoyed his affection she will be entitled to a portion of the inheritance. This despite her not being blood-related and that she will return to her own original family.

d) The inheritance shares are also provided for daughters who are con-sidered as physical part of the deceased and loved by the their father even though, when married, they would leave their parents home and join another family.

e) The recent revamping and improvements have made it possible for the deceased wife and daughters to become recipient of their rightful shares of inheritance. The factors influencing these changes are general acceptance of individual's ownership and, more importantly, the growth and advancement of women's rights, social status and prestige.

The progress of civilization gradually has removed the barriers placed between the genders due to lack of education, proper nurturing and uncaring attention of society. This has led to granting the woman her pride, independence and legal personality as their full rights.

After this introduction the main three topics related to the subject of inheritance will be studied.

1. Drawing a will

Islam has introduced a series of reforms regarding women's social conditions and status, among which is the recognition of woman as an independent owner of her wealth. No man whether her father, her husband, or any of her immediate family has any rights to interfere in a woman's financial affairs whatsoever. As such the woman is empowered and free to make any legal transactions related to any financial contract and for any periodicity. In addition to preparing a will, she is allowed to bequeath and distribute her wealth in any way she desires provided it is within the bounds and in accordance with the general laws of the land.

The French Civil Code would assume a woman to obey her husband, and hence in need of his permission regarding the financial transactions. The law, however, makes an exception on the matter of preparing will by allowing her to be free and have the same rights that her husband enjoys. The rationale for this exception was already explained in chapter ten of Part I. Conversely, in the United States some states (before WWII) did not allow woman to prepare a will without her husband's permission unless such right has been separately contracted between the parties as part of, and in the course of their marriage. In Pennsylvania, New Jersey and Maryland the wife had no rights in her husband's liquid asset. In Massachusetts if the couple had no children the husband inherited one half of her assets and her will was voided regarding this one half. In South American countries, especially the Catholic dominated nations, the rights of the married couple vary with regards to freedom (of the wife) to draw a will.

2. Inheritance of mother and wife
a) Inheritance of mother

The Civil Code of France recognizes four classes of inheritors in terms of relatives, where each class denies it's next generation of class from inheriting; and each class denies the next grade of the class.

The first class includes the children that with their being present there will be no other classes. The second class includes father, mother, brother and sister. One quarter of endowment belongs to each parent. The other half is divided among brothers and sisters. Brothers and sisters like sons and daughters take equal shares. The previous preferential treatment of male over female as well as the eldest to youngest that existed in the old law were removed in the Napoleonic Civil Code. In the event that some children share the same biological parents while some only share one parent the inheritance, allocated to children, is divided in two parts. Those children who share the same biological parent, either their mother or their father, will share equally from one of the two part of the portion; those who share both biological parents, take their shares from both (of the two) parts. If the inheritors consist of the father or the mother and brothers one quarter is allocated to father or mother. If either parent is deceased his or her share is added to brothers shares. If both parents are deceased both of their shares (one quarters each times two) will be added to brothers *and* sisters portion.

The third class includes grand parents and the fourth class includes uncles and aunts families. Here there is an exception to the general rule by partnering the two classes; this has its root from the historical past and was previously mentioned as the wealth of *lower grade* (versus grand). This splitting rule, named after lawmaker *Fente,* basically divides the allocated wealth into two parts; one for the father side inheritors and another for the mother side inheritors. For each division the nearest inheritor to the deceased will take the entire half of the allocated shares for his or her share. Accordingly, the grandfather or the grandmother on the father side will inherit the entire one half of the wealth denying inheritance for the rest of relatives on father side who are farther away (i.e., distanced relative) from the deceased, but they have no effect on the one half allocated to the mother side. This means that grandfather or grandmother will share the entire portion of the wealth, (that was allocated to the third and fourth classes, with cousins, or second cousins, or third cousins, of the deceased[1]). Alternatively grand parents on the mother side may share the inheritance with cousins of the deceased on the father side.

Of course in the case of living parent(s) and grandparent(s) on both sides none of the uncles or aunts and their respective children will have any shares of the inheritance. It is also possible that one or more of inheritors of the second class and one or more of inheritors of the fourth class share the inheritance; meaning the parents of the deceased sharing with uncles and aunts. Hence a father and a cousin on the mother side, or a mother and a cousin on the father side. This matter is also based on *splitting* rule, but here, the article 754 of Civil Code has provided an advantage for parents with the interpretation that either parent will take one half of the inheritance and the other half will belong to cousins, again, either on the father side or the mother side. Additionally, either parent will own one third of the shares of cousins as long as either one is alive.

To sum up: according to the French Civil Code the mother will *not* inherit at all as long as the deceased has a child. If the deceased has brother or sister the mother gets one quarter of the inheritance. If the deceased has only his father or (his) father side relatives the mother will fetch one half and if he has absolutely no relations on father side the mother will have all the inheritance.

According to Islam's Sharia mother is entitled to a share of inheritance even if the deceased has any children. This reflects the homage to motherhood and Islam's interpretation of the principle of blood-sameness. If the deceased has no child the mother's share is one-third of the wealth of the deceased and the rest goes to the father. If there is a child each parent will have one-sixth of the wealth and if the deceased has sister and brother, even though they will not be entitled to any shares, the mother's share is reduced to one-sixth and the father will be entitled to five-sixth. Perhaps the reason for this change, as explained repeatedly, is that only father is expected to provide sustenance for the family. If the inheritors are the mother and one child the mother's share is one-sixth and if there is neither a child nor a father, the entire inheritance will belong to the mother. Regardless of these cases, according to Islam mother is treated as "the first class" of the inheritors and she does inherit from her child's wealth.

b) Inheritance of wife

The older version of Civil Code in France, differentiated between the areas that were influenced by the Romans and the regions whose people had adopted German customs. Those influenced by the Romans allowed the woman to benefit from her deceased husband's inheritance, but those under the influence of the Germans absolutely did not believe in giving such rights to the wife, unless the sharing of inheritance was indicated in their marriage contract. The Napoleonic Civil Code included the wife in the list of inheritors, but only if none of the relative of four classes extended to the 12th generation existed. Since at the time the Civil Code was being compiled the relatives were inheriting through 12th generation the wife was rarely able to inherit any shares from her husband's inheritance. Such inattentiveness towards the rights of women was in sharp contrast with the principle that the French legislators had envisaged in 1804.

It should be noted that the principle of inward affection and love of the deceased with respect to his heirs was followed by French laws of inheritance more than anywhere else. Further, the couple during their married life have the most intimate contact and companionship than any other relatives. With this in mind, when a French governmental consultative body debated on re-structuring and regulating the inheritance law a member of the consultative body, named *Maleville,* proposed to make provisions for a poor and feeble wife to share the family's inheritance now denied by other inheritors as stipulated by law. Another member of consultative body, *Treil Hard,* responded that according to the article 55 one-third of the benefits was already foreseen for the wife. This response satisfied everyone including *Maleville*, but in fact there was no truth to that assertion. *Treil Hard* had mistakenly confused *Maleville*'s proposal with the normal benefit of one-third of inheritance share which would be the right of the deceased parents in case of existence of uncles and aunts. None of the consultative members, government officials, parliament members and senators delved into this matter any further until 1891 when finally a larger portion of inheritance was reserved for the wife.

In the meantime some minor adjustments and corrections were made in this regard. For example, according to the law enacted on 14th July 1866 the woman was given the right to benefit from that portion of her husband's wealth that she had earned through her own labor. The law also enacted on 25th March 1873 allowed the wives to inherit one-half of their husbands earned wealth from living in New Caledonia colony having no child and if they did have a child the wives would inherit one-third of their husbands wealth earned in the colony. The edict of 31st August 1878 further allowed the above-mentioned wife to inherit all the benefits earned from properties that were given to the husband by the government assuming there is no child. If there is at least one child her inheritance is reduced to one-half.

The law enacted on 9th March 1891 made a fixed provision for the wife of the deceased that in any case she would not be deprived from her share of his assets, but since the basis of this inheritance is the existence of companionship and mutual affection for each other the provision makes it contingent upon their *not* being physically separated at the time of the husband's death. Physical separation differs from divorce. Once divorced, there is no longer any affection between the man and the

239

woman and therefore no inheritance. In the case of physical separation, however, the marriage relationship is not yet severed and the couple have not yet been freed from their mutual obligations and neither one is allowed to remarry. Therefore in accordance with the basic rules a physically separated wife is still entitled to her share of husband's inheritance. Nevertheless, the law has denied the rights of the inheritance to either parties because the existence of physical separation tells of indignation and temporary absence of affection between the pair.

According to the law enacted in 1891, if the deceased has no children and no other inheritors all the inheritance with benefits will be inherited by the wife, but if there are other inheritors the wife will only inherit a portion of her husband's inheritance; the measure of such portion is inversely proportional to intensity or weakness of the nearness of relations of inheritors with the deceased in the following manner:

i- In the event there is a child the wife will inherit one-quarter of the inheritance benefits.

ii- In the event the children of the deceased have different mother than the existing one the wife's share will be equal to the share of each child, but it cannot exceed one-quarter of total shares. As an example, if there are four children from another mother then the new wife's share is interpreted as if she was the 5th child, and, as such the wife's share will be one-fifth of total shares. If there are two children one or both of another wife the new wife is assumed to be the second or third child and according to the rule she is entitled to one-half or one-third, but as indicated above, the maximum that she allowed is one-quarter of total shares.

iii- In the event the inheritors are illegitimate children, or legitimate children of an illegitimate child, or brother or sister or parents or grand parents, the wife will inherit one-half of inheritance benefits irrespective of the number of inheritors.

iv- In an effort to improve the status of the wife's inheritance and to per-fect the above-mentioned law (1891), a piece of legislation was enacted on 29th April 1925, prescribing that if there are inheritors other than the ones already named (such as uncles and aunts and their children) the wife will have preferential advantage over all such claims.

Utilizing the inheritance rights, both basic and its side benefits reserved by law for the wife, may prove to be hard to implement. An example would be to find a buyer for the property while the wife is still alive. There is little utility for this arrangement and that is why the law would permit the inheritors to request permission or consent from the wife. In case she refuses inheritors may impose their will; foe example, offering her an annual stipend in return for her cooperation. If no agreement is reached the court will take up the case and will rule in an appropriate manner including the amount that the wife should accept as compensa-tion and its means of guaranteed payment.

Prior to 1917 the rules were such that if a woman remarried (after her husband's death) and the inheritors were the children of the deceased her share of the benefit from inheritance would be voided. There are two reasons for this rationale. First, the woman who is remarried should not be in need of the living expenses and hence no longer distressed. Second, the intent of the law was not to allow the wealth of her ex-husband's family be transferred to her new husband's family. That is because her ex-husband's household functions as long as the children were living in their family home. This topic was yet another facet of collective owner-ship, preventing the spread of the family wealth to outsiders.

Affected by WWI's significant human losses there was an urgent need to facilitate and coordinate a concerted effort in rejuvenation and repro-duction of all European nations and to encourage the widowed women to remarry an incentive was required. One option was to make changes in the inheritance laws to favor widowed women. Subsequently, a law was enacted on 3rd April 1917 that essentially reinstated the woman's right of the inheritance upon her remarriage (after being officially widowed).

It should be noted that as mentioned before there is no limitation in French laws for the family will. There is also no exception between the couple's bequeathing their inheritance. This means that the husband can draw a will bequeathing all the inheritance of his wife's share (that he may inherit) to an outsider[2]; whereas to protect the rights of other inheritors, as noted before, certain portion of the inheritance must be excluded from the will. There is also a possibility that the husband without bequeathing his inheritance to an individual just exclude[3] his wife from receiving her share of inheritance. If the wife has no wealth or other assets and is in need of assistance for her necessary living expenses the law makes provision for allocating a portion of inheritance benefits for her daily expenses. This is the only recourse available to the wife.

As for Islam's Sharia the wife at any event will inherit from her husband's inheritance. If the deceased has a child she is entitled to one eighth and if not she inherits one quarter. In the event there are no other inheritors in accordance to many Islam's jurists the rest of the inheritance would belong to the wife as "refused"(i.e, for other purpose allocation). Regarding divorce if it is revocable (*Raj'i*) and the husband dies during the prescribed period(*Eddeh*), the wife is entitled to her share of inheritance; otherwise she will not be entitled to any inheritance if the link for affection(essential part of marriage) is broken and hence neither one inherits from the other. If the wife has a child from the deceased she has the first right of benefits and all claims on properties' long term leases applicable to the assets. If there is no child some believe she will have no shares in the illiquid assets and she is only entitled to the liquid assets of the deceased with except that she will be entitled to a portion of assessed values of trees and buildings (not of property). Other jurists believe that the wife is deprived only from the land of the property, but not the building and that her rights are the same as other inheritors with respect to the cultivated land and green areas.

242

3. Inheritance of daughter

Western Europe: According to the French Civil Code and civil law in most west European nations the inheritance of sons and daughters of a family is the same; but as mentioned in previous pages, the inheritance was not distributed so equitably in the past centuries; in fact in many cases women had no rights to the inheritance and even today in some civilized parts of the world women are denied their rights of inheritance. In France prior to the Napoleonic Code, that is, until the end of the eighteenth century men enjoyed appreciable advantages over women, and the elders over the younger regarding the inheritance. Daughters[4] except receiving a portion of inheritance from the insignificant, or *lower grade* type of their father's assets without any other rights of inheritance. The "noble" assets and the family assets of father belonged to senior sons. The old custom and traditions of France in regions *Lande* and *Pyrenees* absolutely denied daughters from their father's heritage; the father's assets belonged to the sons only. The Mother's inheritance, however, was equally distributed among the sons and daughters. In England the sons take the priority over daughters with regards to illiquid assets, based on seniority; meaning the eldest son only. Even if the eldest son is deceased his eldest son will be the inheritor. These rules manifest the extreme affection of lawmaker for retaining each family's real-estates and concentrating the power and prestige of senior son of the family who would be the future master of the family estate in all aspects of the family's life.

The Far East: According to civil law of Japan, the daughter's inheritance is insignificant even now. Based on the article 970 the assets of the deceased are divided into those that he himself *inherited* and those that he *acquired* in his life. The inherited assets of her father are reserved for the sons and in their absence, to the second generation, or grade, sons, their grandsons. If there are no sons in any grades the inherited assets would be transferred to sons of the relatives of second and third grades. The acquired assets of the deceased also belong to the sons and only in their absence daughters will become the inheritors. The article 788 of the same law prescribes that a married daughter will belong to her husband's family and shall not return to her original family except if she is divorced. As a result the daughter who resides in her husband's home is denied any inheritance of her blood-relations. A Chinese woman is about to marry receives her dowry in the form of furniture from one of the parents, but she is denied any additional inheritance.

Eastern Europe and Russia: Justinian ordered in 535 that, as in Rome, the status of man and woman would be the same.

In old Armenia, daughters were only given inheritance for which there existed a will.

In Serbia, Moldavia and Greece, before World War I, daughters were denied any inheritance unless there were no sons and then only from what the deceased had acquired during his life. In Hungry, before World war II, the sons' share of the inheritance was three quarters and the daughters received one quarter of the inheritance. In Russia, before the 1917 Russian revolution, daughters were denied any inheritance when there were sons in the family.

Scandinavian countries: The possibility of marriage was based on only the judgement of whoever gave the dowry, that is, the father, the mother, her brother, or the male member of nearest kin and in absence of any a guardian. Daughters only received dowry for their marriage, but no inheritance. Since 1862 an inheritance share for daughter equal to one third of the son was recognized. In 1872 the shares were in parity.

Central Europe: In most areas of Switzerland the sons inherit more than daughters. In *Lioson* and *Zook*, the sons inherit five shares and daughters inherit four shares on father side, but they receive equal shares for the inheritance on the mother side. In Turgi the sons always inherit fifteen percent of the illiquid and five percent of the liquid assets more than daughters. In Freiburg sons inherited twenty percent net in the past, but now they inherit equal share with daughters. In Zurich, until 1855 the daughter inherited one half of the son's inheritance on the father side. Afterwards the equality of shares was established when a majority of people voted in its favor. In *Kenton*, Switzerland household belongings, including the jewelery and decorative items, would belong to the eldest son provided the total value does not exceed five percent of total inheritance; otherwise the excess amount has to be returned as part of the inheritance.

Islam's Sharia categorically states that daughters inherit one half of the share that son receives. In case of only one daughter from the first class of inheritors she will inherit all the heritage (one half as granted and another half as restitution). If there are two daughters all the inheritance will be distributed equally (again, two one-thirds *granted* and the rest as *restitution*). If either one or both parents are alive each would share the inheritance with the daughter(s) one-sixth of total shares will be granted to each parents and depending on one or two daughters one-half or two-third will belong to one or two daughters respectively. The rest, according to different composition will be one-sixth or two-sixth, or nothing at all in the event that both of parents are alive and there would be more than one daughter. In such a case, the parents receive total of one-third (2 x 1/6) and daughters receive (2 x1/3) whereupon no more *restitution* is left. Between the parents and more than two daughters proportional to the first obligation the distribution will be one-quarter or one-fifth, but if the children were sons instead of daughters there would be no restitution left for distribution. After surrendering the obligation for each parent receiving one-sixth, the rest of five-sixth will be divided among all children. Distribution will be made equally if there are all sons, but if children are mixed sons will receive twice the shares that daughters receive.

In summary: Islam has fixed the inheritance share of daughter one half of the son's and that of the wife half of the husband's and that of the sister half of the brother's. The rationale for inequality of the inheritance of man and woman is solely due to the responsibility of sustenance of the family imposed on the man. Thus in contrast to the European civil laws, women have no responsibility for living expenses; nor do they share the living expenses. The wife's responsibility in everyday living is limited to supervision of all non-material related family matters, nurturing and educating the children as well as house chores and not at all requiring any efforts to bring income. At the same time, the observance of principle of blood-sameness, and as always, respecting the prestige and social standing and the rights of the woman in all aspects of life have been the mode of aspiration of Islam's teachings.

Granting a woman inheritance by itself was a daring act by in the 7th century. Islam allowed daughters and wives to inherit from their father's and husband's respectively. Most societies had systematically ignored women from any rights at all, and treating them as non-persons. The reason for their denying women from inheritance was to discourage transfer of wealth from one family to another, which would have been instigated by the marriage of daughters, that would have otherwise diminished the family's total assets.

This concept of denying the woman from inheritance as a means of preventing transfer of wealth had no bearing in Islam's Sharia as related to inheritance because the foundation of Islam's teachings are free from any class distinction. Islam envisioned the formation of a utopian society based on a higher level of understanding and humanitarian ideals.

CHAPTER SEVEN
Assessing the significance and psychology of man and woman

This chapter is devoted to the important topic of evaluating and comparing the significance of social values of male and female. There are several issues that need to be revisited from the perspective of foregoing topics discussed in this book.

First, given the historical past and present references, it may be worthwhile to evaluate whether a woman is physically smaller and weaker than a man hence always influenced by a man. Second, if affirmative, are these characteristics natural and incurable or caused by deficient nurturing and lack of education in the past. Finally can the mental and physical faculties of woman's thought process be strengthened to overcome these deficiencies; thus achieving equality of man and woman in every respect.

Many women have excelled at a particular time and place proving to be better thinkers, more intelligent, more capable and stronger than men.

Nevertheless this does not negate the common belief, held until early 20th century, that in general and in every respect men are expected to be stronger than women and better equipped to bring the opposite sex under their influence History supports that at all times and places and in almost every field of endeavor whether politics, religion, economics, social matters, science, industry, literature and art men have proved to be superior to women and generally maintained a position of leadership. The social significance of this issue is of prime importance.

Some thinkers are of the opinion that "supposed" weakness, deficiency of woman and supremacy of man are all natural and established phenomena that cannot be rectified under any circumstances. To support this claim, they raise several issues regarding the causes for supremacy of man over woman from the beginning of creation of mankind:

- Before the emergence of nurturing and education as factors, what would have happened if no bias was shown.

- In the Beginning, man and woman were free to compete for supremacy and dominance. Why were men given the opportunity to head the family and to dominate social and political power?

- From the early days of creation, man and woman both entered this world with equal footing. Why did woman allow to be subservient to man and obey his orders?

From this point of view, dominance appears to be natural and unalterable. It is further deduced that for certain animals, superiority and dominance do apply. Furthermore scientific research has definitely determined that the weight of the brain and the volume of the heart of man are, sometimes appreciably, larger than that of woman.

In contrast to the above discussion, other researchers and social scholars are of the opinion that indications are that man and woman in the

Beginning were partners and there was no difference in the usage of human beings between them and no specific task was expected from either man or woman. As a result there should be no quantitative and qualitative difference or one being superior to another. Neither is there any difference between the two regarding capability and activity. Any apparent differences may have been caused in the past by external forces in certain areas such as education and training. For this reason, as more effort is made towards training of women, more growth and progress will result which ultimately leads to improvement in social and scientific affairs as well as other aspects of living. Presently, women in the civilized world hold political and social positions. They also represent their countries in foreign lands as well as international forum; they are fully in partnership with men in all aspect of life.

These two topics notwithstanding, there is a third topic which differs from the above two ideas and needs a short explanation.

The structure of the human body is equipped with several key organs which guarantee the continuity of human life. In the event that one of these organs ceases to function human life is disrupted. Each of these organs such as heart or brain or lung or kidney is extremely important; yet it is not possible to rank them in terms of staying alive. This means that all such key organs of the body are equally important. This concept can be extended to other classifications in matters related to everyday functioning of a community. For example, is it possible to choose the most important, or most needed profession among trade artisans, tailors, plumbers or painters? The question is likely to be meaningless because each would serve a particular requirement of daily life. Generally the phrase such as "more important" and "more needed" may not apply at all because they are all ranked the same as far as importance and usefulness. Of course there are certain emergency cases that one particular skill is urgently required; for example, a plumber is most needed when there is a broken pipe, but for any routine daily chores, all skills are equally important and required.

As soon as the basic needs of a person are met such as food and clothing man desires other worldly needs such as visiting recreational public parks to view nature's beauty followed by a need for composing poetry to express such wonders that can only be demonstrated by a poet or a writer who can best describe nature's beauty best. Thus, the existence of both the mastery of words and skill of a plumber are equally needed and important.

It is well known that everyone is endowed with the necessary means for survival. For example nature has provided strong arms for a laborer or a soldier; a sensitive heart to a poet or a writer and a wonderful mind to a philosopher for critical analysis. Everyone's progress and success depends on one's ability to strengthen and to exercise his faculties and talents that nature has provided for him.

After this short introduction it appears that man and woman are two different beings to whom a series of defined and specific tasks are assigned. Such particulars, embedded by nature, are manifested in structural composition of humans' thoughts, mind and body as well as their sensitivity and feelings; hence . This will reinforce the claim of existence of "particulars". These particulars of man and woman carry no advantages of one over another.

All those who perceive that man and woman are composed of the same attributes and made for the same purposes are mistaken; even those who have a reason to evaluate and compare the results in terms of the importance and the value of these two sexes are in error.

The structure of physical, mental, material, intellectual capacity, function, daily tasks and characteristics of man and woman are completely different. Woman is built with distinctive properties and for specific purpose. Man is created for another purpose and in a different fashion. Man is created to fight against external threats and to overcome difficulties and obstacles while actively pursuing independence. Man is created to form a family, earn a sustenance, father a child and protect the woman who, in turn, is created to express compassion, conciliation, affection, feelings, love, being loved, love for others, charm, mother a child, give birth, nurture a child, manage the home where children are nurtured and exercise selflessness and sacrifice; thus man and woman are two entirely different and distinct beings from the perspective of their attributes and characteristics.

Man is made to be an intelligent, prudent, tough, stoic in showing emotions and an opportunist being. As the head of his family he is responsible for earning an income by actively pursuing and amassing wealth; providing family's living expenses and leading his household. Earning a living requires his constant battle against natural hindrances in a world full of conflict and hostility. The necessity of this struggle has made it natural for man to be equipped with such tools as a sound mind, firm resolve, a plan of action, sound thinking and decision making to avoid being influenced by excitement and emotional moods. Nature has planted in a man a strong ego and selfishness as well as a strong drive to ensure that all his daily activities would be consumed around earnings for him and his family.

Woman's life and tasks are different in the world of creation; she is equipped with different tools. She accepts the responsibility of motherhood allowing her to be capable of carrying and giving birth to a child. She is further equipped with unique means of producing nutrition for her child. She then takes an arduous journey towards nurturing her weak offspring who requires protection, support, affection and favor from a stronger individual for a long time. She possesses inherent attributes such as patience and selflessness. In order to overcome the toil of nurturing and hardship of motherhood she is endowed with a soul that takes pleasure from the joy and comfort of others; and their grief affects her more than her own. She replaces selfishness and ego with acts of philanthropy and nourishing.

Lastly, the purpose of creation of woman has been to guarantee the reproduction and continuity of human race. Accordingly, different properties are given to man and woman; each executing his or her assigned specific task to ensure that a perfect match is made. If both man and woman possessed one kind of feeling, affection and temper; it would be impossible for them to live together in harmony while performing different tasks.

In the beginning of creation and prior to any historical precedents man and woman lived freely and under equal conditions. Later on, their positions gradually differed as their characteristics and duties crystalized. Staying home and being excluded from social and political affairs were not, as some have perceived, the result of society's unjust subjugation and disrespect towards women's rights. It is a consequence of following the tradition and the "way" of creation and following the moral soundness of the circumstances of husband and wife as well as prioritizing reproduction. Any variation to this pattern between husband and wife would be considered artificial and unnatural. It will cause disorder in communities and ultimately destabilizes the norm of societies. This is particularly true in most non-western societies.

Woman is specifically responsible for carrying a child, giving birth to a child, nourishing a child, maintaining the home and nurturing the children which is occasionally assisted by her husband. For a mother to additionally undertake all or part of her husband's heavy responsibilities of daily struggle for making a living is quite taxing. She will have to confront stressful conditions in business environments whether commerce, or farming or specialized skills as part of her job in producing income. To accomplish all she would require an extraordinary power beyond the ordinary person. For sure, her everyday tasks would then be more numerous and more difficult than those of man. Woman, therefore, must have been built stronger and more powerful than man. Such conditions would be above and beyond the concept of equality of sexes in terms of abilities and duties, as some thinkers believe.

In conclusion two main issues are of interest. One is that the structured types of, man and woman is different; in principle attempting to measure and compare the two types of humans from the perspective of strength or weakness is meaningless. On the contrary the significance of each type being independent within a defined limit is very relevant. This is equivalent to a merchant and a poet sharing the view of a forest. Each looking, at the huge trees, and evaluating from his point of view. The merchant estimates the potential financial gain in cutting and transporting trees to the market. The poet admires the beauty of nature and views nothing but the charming green and refreshing form of tree branches; he is just fascinated with a beauty of a perfect and an elegant form.

While the merchant is to figure out how the lumber can be extracted from these trees and sold at a good profit to the furniture manufacturers, the poet is concerned about how to derive enjoyment from this idyllic scenery.

In drawing such a parallel, man's nervous system as well as his brain and heart muscles are built for the purpose of activity. He strives to achieve success against constant challenges including natural obstacles. Viewing differently, the body makeup and soul of the woman is associated with esthetic, aroused admiration, gentle heart, mildness, promise of a warm home, giver of birth and nurturer of the children. The able and strong man who returns home from daily travail, enduring hardship in the cold and hot environment, is tired and exhausted. He is home at last, safe and secure. It is the place of comfort and rest for his body and soul. He forgets all the inconveniences and weariness of the day and any traces of sorrow disappears from his memory. His home is the shrine of his desires and his wife is the goddess of his shrine. The young little children are the innocent angels who run around a fireplace warmed by love and purity.

Stars of the universe attract attention for two reasons. They are always glittering and naturally attracting the eyes, but they are also mysterious.

It is largely unknown how and under what circumstances stars were created and hence a mystery. Woman is even a brighter and more mysterious star than heavenly stars. The quality of this enigmatic and mysterious soul is hidden from man; woman is an amazing creature. Constructing a type of fine and delicate being with hidden placement of some contradictory feelings inside her sensitive heart is one of the most incomparable masterpieces of creation. It is not known what affection and contradictory feelings have been placed into this elegant and self conscious soul. Kindness, gentleness, forbearing, conciliation, compassion, faithfulness, holding true, sincerity, grudge, rancor, taking vengeance, discord, deception, jealousy, pride, ego, selfishness and self-adoration comprise only a short list of attributes placed in this mysterious alchemy of creation. The strong-willed and great men with their grandeur and pomp have knelt in front of this beautiful and small creature and have submitted. The Prophet Mohammed constantly expressed his belonging and his loving to one of his wives, *Homira.* The conquerer and a war hero, Napoleon Bonaparte would kneel in front of a woman and would submit to *Josephine* unconditional and powerless.

The first conclusion is, therefore, that the existence of woman is necessary and important and since she is created for performing specific tasks comparison her to man as either superior or inferior has no relevance. It is like quantifying and comparing the properties of two elements, say, steel versus glass and trying to rank one against the other.

The second observation is that a person must be slotted for a specific and appropriate task while keeping in mind the concept of specialization which is now an important ingredient of business success. With respect to man and woman, each should be designated with respect to his or her specialty. No one denies that woman can participate in man's activities, but she does not possess the benefit of the required and naturally developed skills and ingeniousness of man and she will be impeded from her own specialized skills for which man is of no help. This results in breakdown of the system that reproduces and nurtures a regeneration of mankind.

If women instead of engaging in politics, commerce, farming, manufacturing plants, and in many cases plain labor, concentrate on their own duties they will perfect their specialized skills of nurturing and tutoring their children. Concurrently they will organize and manage their family home with optimum results including the issues related to health and education of their community. Such families with high moral standards will be able to educate and deliver brave, strong, responsible and qualified youths for administering and managing many leadership positions in their community; hence a healthy society. The outcome of such society will be manifested in a thousand-fold progress of the nation's economic affairs and its moral values. Still, it should not be left untold that nature has embedded in woman's mental faculty such talents that with proper nurturing and education she could successfully handle any difficult projects whether scientific, industrial, social or political in nature[1]. Yet, the good of society requires everyones best effort to achieve success in his or her own skill and responsibility.

The woman's hardship in carrying a child, giving birth to a child and the continued nurturing of children is no less important than a man who flies over vast oceans, operates equipment that cuts through rugged mountains of breadth-taking height and leads an offensive army in a war front risking counter-attack by the enemy.

Alphabetical Index

Endnotes

PART I

CHAPTER1:

1. Derived from *Res Publica*
2. Notably, *Consuls* (Consulates), *Questeures*(Inquirer), *Edile Curule* (Enforcer, court), their members and *Preteurs Urbains.*
3. Table of 12 principals
4. Proclamation
5. T: The exact period is probably around mid 20th century
6. Known as the prince of "Law Scholars"
7. Known as *Monarchy*

CHAPTER 2:

1. Family Father, Head
2. Family Foyer
3. *Ingenu* (slave)
4. *Affranchis* (freed slave)
5. *Agnatio*
6. *Cognatio*
7. *Patria Potestas*
8. *Peculium Profectis*
9. *Peculium Militaris*
10. *Peculium Quasi-Militaris*
11. *Pecule Advantice*

CHAPTER 3:

1. *Filialoca*
2. *Usus*
3. Here two judges intervene in two instances; first a judge, the Magistrate, investigates the documents and technicalities. If all in order he will provide a summary report to that effect. The second judge, the Judge, who is a layman of good standing and trustworthy acting as an arbiter. It is not necessary for him to be familiar with particulars of judicial procedures, but must be endorsed by both parties. The second judge after investigating the nature of complaint issues his finding which closes prosecution.
4. *Manus injecto*

CHAPTER 4:

1. *Lucius Mestrius Plutarchus* 46 – 120 AD
2. T: His real name is *Odysseys* king of Ithaca
3. Similar to Islam, civil laws in the Uniter Kingdom and France also provide similar credit to eldest son
4. T: In absolute term
5. T: The period is roughly from 17th to 19th century in the west.
6. T: 17th century onward
7. Father, mother, brother, nearest male relative and in absence of any, guardian
8. *Compagne Feministe*

CHAPTER 5:

1. *La Declaration De Droits de L'Homme et du Citoyen*
2. T: Ancestral, meaning social background
3. T: The law enforcer's main job was to protect the nobility and just like security officers they literally watched them as "set before the eyes"

CHAPTER 6:

1. T: since the book was originally published in 1940 the statement about American Indian may be out of date.
2. T: loosely related to gnostic
3. From the book titles "Iran during Sassanid", by Arthur Christensen; *Divaan* means demons and *Izad* is Heaven or God
4. Prof. Christensen's research and other *Iranologists* work indicate that marriage among immediate family members, although allowed, did not appear to be widespread. No particular link is found with either religions of the time, namely Mazda faith or any particular sect of Zoroastrian and contrary to general perception the inclusion of such practices in the culture of ancient communities is not improbable, for this practice in the Iranian culture was the carrier of blood cleansing of relatives and of course, since the "goodness" and "undignified" are relative terms in all societies this tradition was not particularly obscene and shameful.
5. T: Literal text refers to a fire-place exhibiting light which would be otherwise extinguished
6. T: The period is not specified; probably prior to advent of Islam.
7. Italian island in Aegean Sea with population of 22,000.
8. T:Ancient Egypt, 800 km in Mediterranean sea, on the eastern side of Nile, 5th century BC
9. *Salman-e-Farsi*, the close confidant of Prophet describing *Fatemeh* daughter of the Prophet, pale-faced because of her sharing food with the needy people for the past several days; concluding that she wore no veils.

CHAPTER 7:

1. Hist. Univ. des Voy., vol 43, p 362
2. *Sociologie* p. 140 3me, *Aerois*
3. Voy. aux Iles du grand Ocean vol 2 p 496

4.   The Republic of Taiwan

5.   Two of the well known Arab tribes who were sworn enemies; after converting to Islam whereupon, thanks to its teachings, they became allies

6.   *La Sociologie Parle* Dr. Charles *Letourneau*

7.   *La Sociologie* p141

8.   Ibid p135

9.   Livingston missionary travel chapter 28

10.   *La sociologie* p135

11.   Ibid p136

12.   The book of "*Al-meraat and Al -Eslam*" p 8

13.   *Sa'sa'e* is the grand child of *Farazdagh*, the famous poet proudly praises his grand father's act of charity

14.   T: This famous Persian proverb refers to numerous Qur'an verse prohibiting killing of child and that the Creator will provide

CHAPTER 8:

1.   Qur'an verse: ".... We created a match (pair) for you to create peace and tranquility between you as well as love and affection as the foundation of unity."

2.   Although the above definition lacks any social and cultural standing which is the real intent of Islam's Sharia; nevertheless it is clearer than previous laws whether civil or moral and is closer to observing woman's (social) position. In previous laws man was recognized as the sole owner of the woman in marriage. Woman's personality, rights, life, wealth would belong to her husband. In this definition, however, because contracts refer to ownership and owner is indicated as male, yet the man will *not* own anything material-wise that would belong to his wife; except in the form of request which the wife ususally consents to. With respect to woman's wealth and personality and everything else of her, man will have no ownership. He cannot even

force his wife to breast feed the new born child. If she does not agree to do so he must be prepared to hire someone to do so.

3. As much as women are required to treat their husbands with good behavior the men are equally obliged to reciprocate in the same fashion. The Qur'an expressly states: "The belief of one who has a better disposition and behave graciously towards woman is more complete than others. Wish well for your wife and ask for her goodness and well being."

4. T: The second Calif, after the Prophet

5. Qur'an verse 4:21: "Do not make life so unbearable for women that they are forced to give up the material things that were given to them by you (for the price of their freedom). It will not be *halal* for you to take back what you have given to your wife. "

6. Qur'an verse: " God does not waste (the value of) the action of any of His servants, whether man or woman".

7. This topic will be discussed in detail later

CHAPTER 9:

1. *Memoires sur l'Australie*
2. Camile Flammarion philosopher and astrologist
3. Published as *"Contemplations Scientifiques"*, 4th ed. p98
4. Discovered Lake Albert (Tanzania) in 1864
5. Prophet of Islam, as a sign of respect for woman, often held women's stirrup for mounting while kneeling for their convenience
6. The Polynesian islands
7. T: This part of North America refers to now north of Alaska
8. Fitzroy: Voy. *Del'Adventure et du Beagle*,; Darwin: voy. D, un *Naturaliste* p 230; *La Socialogie* 3me ed. p175
9. Camile Flammarion, contemplations *Scietefiques* p101
10. China of early 20th century
11. La Sociologie 3me ed. p183

CHAPTER 10:

1. *Amblyornis Inornata*
2. *La sociologie* p 50

PART II

CHAPTER 1:

1. This kind of distribution is of two types of dividing and multiply-ing. In the first type the animal after maturity is split into two, each as separate being. In the second type the animal after reaching maturity will be equipped with a sheath which is spilt up, from which a lot of bugs will spread out, each as an independent being. Reproduction of microbes falls into one on of the two types.
2. *La Sociologie* 3rd ed. P 236
3. Exogenous
4. T: Late 19th century
5. Endogenous
6. Such as Hottentos and Cafres
7. *La Socilogie* 3rd ed. P 361
8. *La Polyandrie*
9. Sparsely populated islands in gulf of Bengal, Indian ocean
10. *La Sociologie*, Marriage season in Polynesia
11. Qur'an verse: "O' believers, it is not halal for you to abuse a woman by forcefully marrying her just to possess her inheritance."
12. T: This law is probably changed after the 1979 Revolution
13. Similar to Peru, Mexico has a significant pre-colonization of Spain -gained independence in 1828-. Mayas and Aztecs were just some of the civilized tribes of that time; nevertheless the marriage affair never took a general feature of traditions.
14. The first available text of "moral law" compiled 500 years prior to advent of Moses; before then the women of Assyria and Babylon

lived under the most wretched condition. This law improved woman's social status considerably and was practiced until 200 years BC which covered a period of ten centuries after the law was made available. This law contains 282 articles of both civil and criminal rules , 150 of which have been translated to major languages. It begins with punishing act of bribery, followed by describing duties of king's servants with further explanation of rules involving families, marriage and divorce, dowery, inheritance and adoption. Articles 128 to 191 between the time that they were compiled and the Coming of Moses. Three other civilized societies: China, about the same time as *Hammurabi;* India about 11th century BC; and Egypt in the same century as *Hammurabi* laws were compiled for managing the man and wife relationship as well as the rules governing the family foundations. These law books were in 8 volumes placed in Pharaoh palaces.

15. Islam also prohibits selling of slave woman who is the mother of her child.

16. Although the spread of civility throughout the world has almost eliminated this type of marriage among primitive groups and the woman's elevated social status does not allow such humiliation; yet sadly, the practice in advanced societies such as France and U.S., where freedom of association between man and woman, and its meaning in civility, are misinterpreted so that experimental associations are increasingly becoming a de-facto marriage between man and wife, similar to what is practiced in Sri Lanka. The young man claiming that they need to know all the particulars of his future wife and as soon as his lust has subsided he finds an excuse to severe the relationship avoiding the real marriage.

17. T: Late 19th century

18. *La Sociologie* 3rd ed. P 352

19. Ibid

20. *Loud Falies Etude Histoire et Philos suries civilisations* Tome 2' P 398

21.   Voy *aux iles du Grand Ocian* Tome 2' P 484-503
22.   *La Sociologie* 3rd ed P 371
23.   Iran's civil laws have made no specific reference to this matter, albeit breaking of any conditions indicated in marriage contract would give a cause to man to have a choice for termination.
24.   *La Sociologie* 2nd ed P 353
25.   Qur'an verse 4: 22 " If you desire to take a wife instead of another and you have given one of them a treasure do not take anything back from her. Do you do so by unfounded accusation, a sin?"

CHAPTER 2:

1.   Qur'an verse: " ..if there are those who are poor God will provide from his [unlimited] resources".
2.   Qur'an verse:7:190 " Creation of man and wife is from a single source (soul): between the two of them is placed love and mercy"
3.   Qur'an verse 8:25 "...We placed love and mercy between the man and wife..." is interpreted as freedom of choice is assumed for either party equally.
4.   Jozam Ansari
5.   Abi-Lebabet-ibn-Abdol-Monzar
6.   Omar-ibn- Khattabb
7.   Qur'an verse: ".. discuss in kindly and good nature the differences with one another .."
8.   Based on the phrase from the Quran verses: The father is built stronger physically and mentally than mother"
9.   Refer to Chapter 5: Divorce
10.   At the same time, Islam has not denied the right of women to engage in social affairs.
11.   Recent rulings allow either parents' consent.
12.   In other words, polygamy and marrying while not divorced from the first wife is prohibited.
13.   Forbidden marriage of immediate family includes 4th generation.

14. Since the nature of this is considered personal particular, it falls in the category couple's nationality jurisdiction.

15. These activities began after WWII

16. These restrictions have been removed since 1938

17. Article 311 of French Civil Code, which is a continuation of the enacted law of February 1819, interprets physical separation as a kind of minor divorce. Since a physical separation, in most cases, resembled real divorce and ultimately led to divorce; therefore it is a divorce in so far as woman's independence is concerned and subsequently returning woman' full rights

18. It is well known that in other transactions, an individual not being of legal age is a cause for disqualification of the and therefore "relative" voiding of contract is in effect The contract can be reinstated once the legal age is reached. This is particularly applicable to case that the couple marry without the permission of their parents. In the case of marriage, however, because of marrying a person who is not of legal age and public disorder is created. In this case the voiding of contract cannot be reinstated once the party reaches the legal age.

19. After the completion of ages fifteen and eighteen respectively

20. Financial contract should not be confused with marriage contract

21. Regarding the historical root of this method in France, there are different opinions among the scholars. Some Roman laws are based on the belief that the source is a definition presented in the book " Digest" in which there is joint benefit for the couple and the husband has the right to manage the wife's wealth in any way that he would consider benefitting the family. Some believe the law is derived from Celtic laws, practiced in the *Gauls* regions, because Julius Caesar, the conquerer of Gauls, had determined that the husband had set aside equivalent to wife's dowery(from his wealth), collectively saved for children future; the income of which was not to be spent , but was re-invested for the sake of their future. Others, yet, believed that the source is Germanic since the Germans had reserved one-third of joint wealth for the

wife who survived her husband. Finally, others believed that the source was completely French based on local customs of people of various regions of France based on correct reasoning and family love and affection. They discovered that the best way of uniting interests of the couple in its true sense was to share the their wealth. As a result, this method when adopted as a generally accepted form of financial contract is now practiced all over the country.

22. As discussed before, the dissolution of joint wealth does not necessitate dissolution of marriage contract and it is possible that court would intercede by splitting the wealth of the couple while still married.

23. Although in accordance with definition of joint or shared wealth all the liquid assets of the couple whether incorporated before or after the marriage, and neither one should possess private account; nevertheless they can agree to keep any liquid assets that either one has received as gift- excluded from the joint wealth.

24. Action *Paulienne*

25. Benefice d' Emoluement

CHAPTER 3:

1. T: The author of this book. The author often refers to Christianity without any specific denomination. In particular, regarding marriage his reference should be directed to Catholicism and practice of celibacy.

2. T: The book was written during the WWII reflecting Europeans heavy population losses

3. The latest Iranian law of "Family Protection" enacted in 1967 has left the matter of polygamy subject to court ruling and only contingent on special circumstances.

4. T: The question is if a man can whole-heartedly "love" four women at the same time.

CHAPTER 4:

1.   *Rien ne Nous rend si Grana q'une gande douleur*

CHAPTER 5:

1.   Separation de corps
2.   Nequet
3.   Fourteen hundred years ago, Islam's advanced laws had equally prosecuted, convicted and punished man and woman for adultery,; whereas according to French criminal law even today (1970's) penalty for man is monetary, but woman will go to prison. Recent changes since the date of publication have corrected the deficiencies.
4.   Because the party is either an abuser, or adulterer or convicted felon who in any case is not qualified to care for the child.
5.   For more information refer to chapter 3, part II
6.   As mentioned above
7.   According to Islam Sharia dementedness of either spouse gives the right to cancel the contract to the other party.
8.   This condition is not valid if the woman is free from menstrual or carrying a child; also if the husband has been absent long enough that his wife's monthly period has moved to another has occurred in which case free from menstrual discharge is meaningless.
9.   Because there is no marriage contract as yet.
10.   Book titled "*Almara*' fee Islam p 37
11.   The *Parade* magazine
12.   *Tahrir-el-mara*', *Ghasem Amin Beik*, p183
13.   The latest laws (in Iran) have clarified this issue making it easier to apply for women wanting to divorce
14.   All Muslim countries that desire to harmonize their civil laws in accordance with Islam's Fegh *can incorporate Osr-o-haraj principle for woman to force her husband for divorce when*

she meets the conditions described by Osr-o-haraj. The entire French and other countries laws related to right of woman to divorce are based on the principle of *Osr-o-haraj* fully in compliance with the spirit of Islam.

CHAPTER 6:

1.   Until 1918, according to France's Civil Code the cousins both on mother side and father side up to 12th generation will inherit from the deceased and the rest will belong to the State. On December 31, 1918 the government proposed and the parliament approved that the inheritance be limited to 4th generation. This was later modified to the 6th generation by the Senate.
2.   Equal for man and woman, albeit since protection of women's rights is focused no mention is made of man's The rulings applied to wife's inheritance equally apply to husband's and in general all distributions of inheritance rights.
3.   This particularity of freedom and limitless bequeathing of man and wife to each other is derived from France's laws principle of mutual love between the deceased and the survivors.
4.   The portion which the deceased acquired while alive.

CHAPTER 7:

1.   The capability of late Mrs Nehru, the Prime Minister of Subcontinent of India is testimony to this assertion.

General note: "T" indicates translator's comment

www.ingramcontent.com/pod-product-compliance
Lightning Source LLC
Chambersburg PA
CBHW071401170526
45165CB00001B/144